MW00769770

The Book of
PROVERBS

Titles from Kevin Swanson

Family Bible Study Guides
Genesis: A Family Bible Study Guide
Psalms I: A Family Bible Study Guide
Psalms II: A Family Bible Study Guide
Psalms III: A Family Bible Study Guide
Proverbs I: A Family Bible Study Guide
Proverbs II: A Family Bible Study Guide
Proverbs III: A Family Bible Study Guide

Christian Curriculum Project
Christian Classics Study Guide — Senior Level
Christian Classics Study Guide — Junior Level
Great Christian Classics: Five Great Narratives of the Faith
What Does the Bible Say About That?

The Second Mayflower
Upgrade: 10 Secrets to the Best Education for Your Child

The Second Mayflower Audiobook
Visionary Manhood (MP3 / CD)
Vision for Generations (MP3 / CD / DVD)
Reforming the Church in the 21ˢᵗ Century (CD)
Family Economics Conference Audio Series (MP3 / CD)
Family Economics Conference Video Series (DVD)

The Book of

Proverbs

God's Book of Wisdom

BOOK 2: PROVERBS 16–23

Kevin Swanson

GENERATIONS *with* VISION

Copyright © 2011 by Kevin Swanson
Printed in the United States of America
Second printing, 2012

ISBN: 978-0-9826298-8-8

Scripture quotations are taken from the
King James Version
All rights reserved

Published by
Generations with Vision
10431 South Parker Road
Parker, Colorado, 80134
www.generationswithvision.com
For more information on this and
other titles from Generations with Vision,
visit www.generationswithvision.com or call 1-888-839-6132.

CONTENTS

INTRODUCTION

When my wife and I set out to educate our children at home, we were confused by the hundreds of theories on the education of children that were presented at homeschool conventions. Parents who love their children really want to find the best *paideia*, or education, for their children, and we were no exception to that rule. So it was always with some frustration that we would attend the next seminar on yet another philosophy or technique of education. Eventually, we turned back to the Word of God.

Our first assumption, of course, is that God is very smart. Assuming that it is He Who is behind the marvelous design we call the "human being,"—and anyone who can create things like human beings has to be, well, *smart*—we turned to His Word. Thankfully, He didn't leave us without operating instructions. But, like most fathers who try to assemble a toy on a child's birthday and usually turn to the manufacturer's instructions as a last resort, most people do the same thing when trying to figure out how to operate a human being. Finally, I picked up the Word of God and looked up the word "education" in the concordance. Naturally, the Bible doesn't have much to say about things like schools and education. But I broadened my search to "knowledge," "understanding," and "wisdom," and found that God has actually dedicated an entire book of the Bible to the subject of transmitting knowledge, wisdom, and understanding to a child. This book—Proverbs—is Education/Knowledge/Wisdom 101, authored by God and conveyed by Solomon, who was endowed with supernatural wisdom by God Himself. This gives us both the method and content of a child's education. It is a textbook for young men (and young women), providing the basic corpus of knowledge God requires of young people.

Now one of the things that takes many educators by surprise is that the Book of Proverbs does not have a great deal to say about geography, geometry, or geology. So why would the Creator of the Universe—Who, as I mentioned, is very smart—neglect something as important as the Pythagorean Theorem in His textbook? I submit that it is because geometry, in the grand scheme of things, is not all that important. When it comes to the education of a child, faith and character are primary in God's estimation. These are the warp and the woof of the *paideia* of a child if we are speaking of the Lord's nurture and admonition (Eph. 6:4). They constitute the foundation, the studs, and the drywall in the "construction of a child." And geometry, geography, and geology are only the wall paper. Attempting to teach geometry apart from character is akin to trying to place wallpaper on walls that do not exist, which would be a prime example of an "exercise in futility."

As you read this book, you will learn God's basic truths, addressing the classical philosophical divisions of epistemology, metaphysics, and ethics. You will grapple with the tensions of determinism and human responsibility. You will find an entire system of priorities for life's ethics and purposes. You will find the basic constituents of a biblical social system, as well as principles for sound economics, government, and general business management. The book gives insight into the proper views of theology, anthropology, and human psychology. Any education program will give you a categorical system by which you can understand life, history, truth, ethics, and reality. Some systems have a semblance of truth, but all will fundamentally be compromised if they do not begin with the Book of Proverbs and the fear of God (Prov. 1:7).

Having taught in public and private schools, and seeing myself as an academic of sorts, I was at first uncomfortable with the Book of Proverbs. A pastor once told me that there are those who teach faith, character, the fear of God, and then there are those who teach reading, writing, and arithmetic; according to his viewpoint, those who teach the Book of Proverbs are not the same as those who teach chemistry and mathematics. But as time went on, I became convinced that Christians must not tolerate this dualism. This separation of the fear of God from the chemistry class has produced an ungodly, secular science and yielded its terrible destruction in our "brave new world." The separation of the fear of God from social studies and political science has undermined the Christian foundations of this country and created tyranny (Prov. 28:2; Neh. 5:15). I place the blame for the failure of the Christian faith in the West, the widespread apostasy, and the breakdown of our Christian institutions at the feet of those who separate the knowledge of chemistry and political science from the fear of God. Christian chemistry teachers should be less interested in their students learning chemistry as they are in their students *learning the fear of God through chemistry* (Prov. 1:7, 23:17). Thus, we do not separate discipleship from education—or the fear of God from "academic subjects." The same principle applies to Christian parents.

The Book of Proverbs is presented by "Solomon the son of David, king of Israel. . . to give subtilty to the simple, to the young man knowledge and discretion" (Prov. 1:1–4). Therefore, every college in America—certainly every Christian college—should require its students to memorize the Book of Proverbs because it is God's book on the education of every young person. It is God's theory of education, presenting both content and methodology in living color. If teaching colleges took up this theory, they would be effectively training future fathers and mothers to teach their children the lessons of life. Reading through the Book of Proverbs, you can practically hear the writer's exhortations, warnings, and instructions, filled with urgency, tenderness, severity, passion, and love. They may not fit in well with the professional teaching methodology you will learn in teaching colleges, since those theories have incorporated more from men like Dewey, Rousseau, and Plato than they have from the Christian God.

The Core Curriculum

As I considered these things, I became deeply convicted that my children were better-educated in Saxon Math and the laws of grammar than they were in the Book of Proverbs. They did not know the many lessons found in the Book of Proverbs. So, over the subsequent ten years, I set about the task of expositing, illustrating, and applying every verse in the Book of Proverbs four times through. I assembled those lessons into this Proverbs Family Bible Study Guide with the hope that others might benefit from my efforts.

In our education program for our children, this book is the core, setting the stage for all other academic subjects they pursue. It will prepare them well for any and all of their economic and "career" pursuits. But it will give them far more than this. It will prepare them for their own family discipleship program, for relationships within the church, and for a living, vital walk with God. By the time my children leave my home, I want them to be familiar with every verse of this book.

God's Book on Life Is for Everyone

Genesis is God's history book of the world, the Book of Psalms is God's book on worship, the Gospels are God's autobiography of the Savior, and the Book of Proverbs is God's book on life. Every child raised in a Christian family should be thoroughly versed in this book before leaving home. But also, when discipling any person into the Christian church for the first time—after teaching them the Gospel of Matthew and the book of Genesis—I would recommend a complete study of the Book of Proverbs for the *catechumen,* or disciple. The Great Commission requires teaching others to observe and practically apply every command of Christ to their lives. God's book of wisdom and life must never be neglected in this task.

Using This Study Manual

This Study Manual includes modern day applications and illustrations to help illuminate the meaning of the text. It also provides helpful family discussion questions to open up more shepherding opportunities for Dad and Mom. Of all of the books of the Bible, the Book of Proverbs will lead to the most family discussions regarding the application of God's truth to everyday situations and problems.

I recommend reading the Bible text in unison as a family before Dad or Mom reads the exposition and application questions. It is also a good idea to end each lesson with another reading of the text, in order that everybody will remember the lesson. Each proverb is packed with weighty considerations, making it worthy of careful thought and meditation throughout the day.

You may also wish to memorize the verse together, as our family does. First, we repeat the verse three times together. Then, each child has an opportunity to say the verse, with Dad or Mom correcting as they go. Each time a family member recites the verse, the others should be encouraged to recite it silently in their minds. By the time everyone has recited the verse, all should be able to say it together in unison, without error. We have used this method of memorization since we first learned it from Pastor Henry Reyenga about five years ago, and it has worked marvelously for our family.

For the biblical text I have used the classic King James Version with only minor changes, replacing "thee" and "thou" with "you" and "your," and changing the older verb forms (for example, changing "seeketh" to "seek").

PART 110 ~ GOD, THE SOURCE
Proverbs 16:1

The preparations of the heart in man, and the answer of the tongue, is
from the LORD.

Some proverbs are more difficult to understand than others,
and almost every English version of this particular verse yields
a different translation of the Hebrew text. Thankfully, this is
not true of the corpus of God's Word. So if we hold this verse
under the light of the rest of the Word which is both clearly
translated and generally understood, we can extract the truth
out of it.

As in the case of the prophet Balaam, who could not say
a single thing except what God permitted him to say, so
here the wise man claims God to be always in control of
the tongue. This applies to everything that is said by every
person, speaking in every language on the earth. Even wicked
men may say many wicked things, but God will be sure that
they say the "right" evil thing! God is neither the author of
sin nor the architect of the wicked hearts of men. Yet, there
will be no wicked thing said or wicked action taken but that
which is ordained by God Himself. When the wicked Jews
cried out to Pilate those wretched words, "Crucify Him!" and
by wicked hands turned their Messiah over to the Romans
for crucifixion, their actions came by the full intent of the
determinant counsel of God (Acts 2:23). Even as God has a
higher purpose operating through the evil actions and words
of men—such as in the case of the atoning death of His Son
for the sins of His people—man is still responsible for those
actions. This is because the sinful nature of the event is a
consequence of the ruminations and motivations of the heart.
God's heart is pure in all that He orchestrates. However, man's
heart is evil, and it is the evil in men's hearts that makes them
culpable before God for their sin.

Proverbs 16:2

All the ways of a man are clean in his own eyes; but the LORD weighs the spirits.

Men hate to think that they are either lacking in moral virtue or failing to meet the standard of absolute ethics. So they institute their own standards. It doesn't matter whether a man is just an ordinary nice guy raising four kids in the suburbs or a serial murderer in a maximum security prison—even cannibals have their standards of moral decency as they remind their children to wipe their mouths with a banana leaf after consuming human flesh. *All the ways of a man are clean in his own eyes.* He may even have to shift his standard on a regular basis in order to stay up with the depravity of his own inclinations and practices. Regardless, he remains the absolute (yet shifting) standard of what is right and wrong; for as long as he rejects Yahweh God as the Lawgiver, he must fulfill that role as his own god.

Yet, God exists. A man may play the charade for a lifetime, but God is still in the heavens, and He is watching and judging. Indeed, every work of man is weighed in the balances of justice that are calibrated to one-billionth of an ounce. Every hypocrisy, every inequitable metric of judgment imposed upon others, and very work of unrighteousness are placed on the balance and carefully weighed against the standards of God's holy law. May God help us to see things from His perspective and acknowledge Him to be the standard of what is right! And may He enable us to receive Jesus as both our Savior and our King!

Proverbs 16:3

Commit your works to the LORD, and your thoughts shall be established.

When a man commits to walk in God's ways and then takes real steps in that direction, his thoughts and perspectives begin to change. In other words, right action produces clear, right thinking. Some things are hard to explain in words. Take love, for example. When a man travels 5,000 miles to serve in an orphanage, he begins to understand a little bit more about what Jesus did when He navigated a universe to serve and sacrifice Himself for a raggedy bunch of sinners like us. Moreover, a man hardly knows what true forgiveness is until he has forgiven a persecutor who has subjected him to horrible beatings and torture. When we handle things the way God wants us to handle them, we begin to see things the way God sees them.

Instead of signing up for three years of seminary in order to "learn" all the stuff you need to learn about God, it might be just as useful to ask God every day what He wants you to do today. How does He want you to spend your money? What are His priorities? How can you love somebody in a concrete way? Commit your works to the Lord, and your thoughts will be established.

Family Discussion Questions:

1. What standard do we use to measure our own thoughts, words, and behavior? How often do we go back to the Word of God and compare our lives to this holy standard?

2. Give several examples of how you might set out to do something in order that you might understand some truth found in God's Word.

PART 111 ~ HOW GOD SAVES US FROM EVIL
Proverbs 16:4

The LORD has made all things for Himself: yea, even the wicked for the day of evil.

This is a biblical view of the problem of evil. Every worldview or religion must wrestle with the nature and cause of evil. All but the Christian worldview must minimize it or just dispense with the idea of evil altogether. We acknowledge evil, the source of which is the hearts of men. But how can

God still be the cause of what becomes evil effects and yet be innocent of sin? Herein lies a great mystery. Put another way, how can God be all good and all powerful, and yet evil still exists in the world? Wouldn't a good God wish to purge all evil, and shouldn't His power be sufficient to prevent it? The wisest mere man who ever walked this planet answers this extraordinarily difficult conundrum with this one simple statement: "Yahweh has made all things for Himself: yea, even the wicked for the day of evil." The problem of evil is no logical contradiction for us when we append an additional premise to the syllogism: "God has a morally acceptable reason for the evil that is in the world."

Either evil has somehow frustrated or confounded the purposes of God, and He is no longer God, or God is still God, and He is still sovereign over evil. There is no middle ground on this. The wicked and the wicked things they do are all still part of the purposes of God.

Everything that is made is made for God's purposes and for God's glory. They will serve His interests and His purposes. Some will serve willingly here and now, yet others will find themselves working out God's purposes unwittingly. When God's justice is finally satisfied in the judgment of some wicked man, his entire life, death, and judgment will bring God glory, working for His purposes.

As we contemplate these deep truths, we would do well to remember that there is no evil on earth to be feared. Oh that we would fear only God every day!

Proverbs 16:5

Every one that is proud in heart is an abomination to the LORD: though hand join in hand, he shall not be unpunished.

The pride of men is the fundamental sin that undermines all fear of God and submission to every one of His commandments. Since Adam and Eve succumbed to the first temptation in the garden, men have turned themselves into little gods, insisting that they will define what is good and evil or right and wrong.

It is only when we admit that God is the One Who makes the rules and humbly confess our own failure to comply with His laws that pride is overcome in our own hearts and lives. But for those who are too stiff-necked and proud to confess their sins, and for those who perpetually justify themselves and cast blame on others, they will have to face the terrible prospect of God's disapproval and condemnation.

Sometimes proud men will combine forces against the Lord and against His Anointed, the Lord Jesus. Perhaps their consciences remind them that no rational man can pretend to be god in open opposition to the God Who created the heavens. So, consciously or unconsciously, they form their secret societies, godless coalitions, international banking cartels, and even world governments. But they are still pretending! This is just as irrational as if they were trying to oppose God all by themselves. If an ant were to create a campaign against a human being, it would be hard to imagine how even 10,000 ants acting in coordination might be able to overcome a human armed with a couple of ounces of pesticide. This example is barely comparable to God's relationship with the creatures that populate the third rock from the sun in a galaxy of a billion suns. Conspiracies may stand for a century or two, but He that sits in the heavens shall laugh until His anger is kindled just a little—and then He will utterly crush the conspirators once and for all.

Proverbs 16:6

By mercy and truth iniquity is purged: and by the fear of the LORD
men depart from evil.

What a wonderful summary of the Gospel is found in this little nugget of truth! The deep stain of sin besmirches God's world, sinks us in a sea of guilt and misery, and brings ruined relationships, destruction, and death. Although the godly men and women of the Old Testament obediently sacrificed thousands of animals, circumcised millions of men and boys, and coated temples, altars, and themselves with bloody remnants of slain beasts, none of that was sufficient to wash them clean of the deep, dark stains of sin that contaminated their souls. It is only by means of God's mercy and God's truth that such stains could ever be purged away. As we preach and teach the Word to our children each day, over the years we see their hearts and lives purged of selfishness, strife, envy, anger, pride, and covetousness. The Word scrubs and scrubs, and slowly—sometimes imperceptibly—the regenerating, sanctifying effects of the Word appear in their lives. But it is more than the preaching of the Word. Without the concomitant work of the Spirit of God mercifully applying the blood of Jesus to the hearts of our little ones, there would be no spiritual life whatsoever.

But what do we say to men who tell us they are Christians but they cannot quit sinning? They may be hopelessly addicted to serving the alcohol god, or they may habitually react in anger when things don't go their way. They have yet to learn an important lesson of the biblical, Christian faith. According to Revelation 14:6, they have yet to learn the Gospel. It is by the fear of the Lord that men will depart from evil. Are you having trouble departing from evil? You obviously must be having trouble with this foundational matter of fearing God.

More often than not, children who are not honoring their parents have forgotten the God Who deputized their parents to train them in His Word. We fear the police officer who pulls us over on the highway only because he is deputized by the state and has all of the judicial systems, weaponry, and authority of the state behind him. Should our children fail to recognize the Ultimate Authority who deputized their parents and established their authority to act in His behalf, it is doubtful they will demonstrate much honor for their parents.

Family Discussion Questions:

1. How have we seen sin and iniquity purged from our home over the years?

2. How does the fear of God destroy the death grip of sin in our lives?

PART 112 ~ GOD IS SOVEREIGN
Proverbs 16:7

When a man's ways please the LORD, He makes even his enemies to be at peace with him.

All of the relationships we cultivate with relatives, coworkers, neighbors, and church members can make our lives very complicated. But it doesn't have to be that way because only one relationship is of real importance at all times—our relationship with God. Are we ever afraid of what people think about us? Perhaps a neighbor is contemplating a lawsuit against us, or a relative refuses to speak to us for some reason or another. Any of these things could bring great consternation, fear, and worry into our lives. Yet a true man of faith will always return to his relationship with God. He will ask himself, "How has my behavior in this relationship been offensive to God? What have I done that may be distancing the Holy Spirit from me at this time?" As the old saying goes, "It's impossible to keep everybody happy with you all of the time." If you are a man of principle and action, you will make some people unhappy by your perspectives and decisions. It is inevitable. Therefore, as you strike out into life, you should chart a course that is most pleasing to the God you serve. Heed the Spirit-filled, godly counsel that directs you in the will of God, but ignore the flak, the torpedoes, and the detractors that would sway you from your course. In the end, God will make sure that your enemies keep their distance and maintain relative peace with you.

The same principle may be applied to nations. Think of all the complex political maneuverings, negotiations, preemptive measures, and wars that could be avoided if national leaders would pay attention to this simple lesson. *When a man's ways please the Lord, He makes even his enemies to be at peace with him.* There are a thousand potential enemies crossing our borders each day; terrorism is on the rise, and rogue states have more access to weapons of mass destruction than ever before in history. No political leader could ever apply enough wisdom, diplomacy, or security measures to preempt all of the possible threats on a nation. But when a nation's ways please the Lord, He makes their enemies to be at peace with them! The presidents and judges of nations would do well to set their priorities by the laws of God. Instead of focusing attention upon the threats to national security, they ought rather to take care of the government-endorsed mass shedding of innocent blood within their own borders. They ought to address the problem of trillions of dollars of government money poured into godless educational systems that train hundreds of millions of young people to not fear God in science, origins, history, and letters. This is the best state policy of all. Please God in the internal affairs of the nation, and He will take care of the department of state!

Proverbs 16:8

Better is a little with righteousness than great revenues without right.

One of the fundamental problems with modern life is that we fail to live by the priorities of God's Word. If you do not understand God's priorities, you will consume precious time and resources on the wrong things, thereby failing to live the good life as defined by God Himself. Unfortunately, this is the legacy of much of modern life which seeks after material well-being while neglecting God's desires for our lives. How many times does a father place his money-making efforts over the spiritual needs of his family? As men fail to exhort their families daily, and then increasingly neglect the assembly of the saints on the first day of the week, you will see the faith dying out in their generations.

If you ever have an opportunity to trade money for righteousness, take advantage of such a deal. A man should never compromise his integrity for money in business or in politics. Money seems as if it will provide us more impact and more influence for good, but righteousness doesn't always need money for its cause to prevail. Recently, conservative Christians entangled themselves in a gambling lobby that provided them funds for their political campaigns—all for the cause of family values and righteousness, of course. But what they forgot was that the commodity that really matters in life is righteousness, and money is only useful as far as it is used in the cause of righteousness.

Proverbs 16:9

A man's heart devises his way: but the LORD directs his steps.

God is sovereign. This is among the most basic defining statements in the Christian faith. Failure to acknowledge the sovereignty of God is failure to acknowledge the "God-ness" of God. But such statements as these are terribly insulting to humanist man who wants to see himself as the hinge point of reality, the ultimate determinant of what happens.

But it should be clear enough that the future is indeterminable for us, in the ultimate sense. If I were to plan doing something tomorrow, any one of ten thousand things might happen that would frustrate my plans, and there is no way that I could prevent all of these possible contingencies from happening. For instance, a meteorite might hit my house and kill me. A police officer might arrest me and throw me in prison for a week or two, or I might lock my keys in my car and be unable to drive where I had intended to go. Only a sovereign God could possibly control all of these contingencies. This is why James cautions us to preface our plans to do such and such with the caveat, "If the Lord wills" (James 4:15).

These reminders should keep us forever humble, for we have no ultimate control over our lives. Only God is in total and absolute control over tomorrow.

Family Discussion Questions:

1. Do we spend more time thinking about what others think about us, including those who might consider themselves our enemies, or what God thinks about us?

2. Have you ever had an opportunity to trade money for righteousness? Give examples of where and how this might occur.

3. If God can short-circuit our plans anytime He wants to, how should this change our outlook on the future?

PART 113 ~ LEADERSHIP
Proverbs 16:10–12

A divine sentence is in the lips of the king: his mouth transgresses not in judgment.

A just weight and balance are the LORD'S: all the weights of the bag are His work.

It is an abomination to kings to commit wickedness: for the throne is established by righteousness.

To understand the Bible, you need to know the difference between the *descriptive* and the *prescriptive*. The descriptive merely describes what *is* the case, while the prescriptive presents what *ought* to be the case. When we say that a man robbed a bank we are merely describing what a man did. When we say that a man *ought not* to rob a bank, we move into the arena of the prescriptive. When reading Scripture, it is important to determine whether the Bible is describing, recommending, or commanding an action.

Now then, what may be said about the present text? Is it descriptive or prescriptive? Sometimes the Bible will equate what is and what ought to be the case by failing to make any clear distinction. Here we learn either that the king judges righteously, or that he should judge righteously, but which is it? Verse 12 explains further. The throne of a civil ruler is established in righteousness. A king should and must judge righteously, and as he makes righteous judgments, he fulfills the definition of a king. To the extent that he fails to do this, he undermines his own right to rule and the authority of his own position. It's just that simple. If a king were to allow anarchy to prevail as he failed to prosecute criminals, he would forfeit his right to rule. Over a period of time, his dynasty would fall, and his empire would break down. This doesn't mean that every king rules with perfect judgment. When he fails to judge righteously, he fails, at that moment, to act in a "kingly" way. This principle applies to fathers, elders, judges, legislators, and presidents.

Man by nature always falls back into tyranny and anarchy because he gravitates away from the righteous standards of God's law. It is only God's law that provides any true law and order to a land. Some countries prosecute crimes of theft and murder. Some will prosecute crimes of adultery, abortion, and homosexuality. Typically, kings and judges will not want to prosecute crimes that they commit! This should be intuitively obvious. But when a nation is filled with murder, abortion, homosexuality, and fornication to such an extent that even the leaders commit such crimes, the basic order of the nation unravels into anarchy again.

Thus, you can see how the character of kings and leaders are important. They are, in a real sense, the last defense to the undoing of a nation. When a father, pastor, or leader gives in to moral failure, the repercussions upon the people they lead are severe. It is truly an abomination to kings to commit wickedness.

Fundamental to a stable society is an honest means of market exchange. When cheating prevails either on the part of "the little guy" or by huge banking cartels that find ways to debauch the currency, entire economic systems will fail. The God Who claims honest weights and balances for His Own will never bless an alien system of economics that constantly manipulates the value of money for the benefit of some select institutions or persons.

For related commentary, reference Proverbs 11:1.

Proverbs 16:13

Righteous lips are the delight of kings; and they love him that speaks right.

Here we find another mark of "kingliness," or, more generically, good leadership. The best leaders are attuned to both recognize and appreciate wise and righteous words. No leader in his right mind likes to be lied to. In fact, one of the most basic laws governing competent leadership calls for a ready and open ear for "bad news." Those who are willing to hear the bad news first are usually prepared to react to it in a balanced, wise, and a righteous way. Bad things happen to everybody, to every organization. Leaders want to hear the truth, even if it is a negative report. But that's not all. There are too many people in the world who want to complain fruitlessly about all the problems, crime, and evil in the world. Good leaders won't tolerate these tirades. They also want to hear righteous, honest, and creative solutions to the problems.

Proverbs 16:14–15

The wrath of a king is as messengers of death: but a wise man will pacify it.
In the light of the king's countenance is life; and his favour is as a cloud of the latter rain.

A song from the 1960s had a grain of truth in it when the rebel conceded, "I fought the law and the law won." Of all of the unprofitable things that men allow to consume their lives, there is nothing as useless as picking a fight with a police officer or a civil judge. This is not to say that we don't employ legal means to avert judicial injustices. Remember that the Apostle Paul himself appealed to Caesar to avoid an early demise at the hands of his Jewish brothers. But, even in the throes of injustice and persecution, a Christian will respectfully and patiently appeal to the leader's better sense of goodwill and justice. After all, any leader worth his salt knows that he must uphold some semblance of justice if he wants to retain his position and prevent total anarchy from breaking out.

Family Discussion Questions:

1. If righteousness is what establishes authority in civil government, how might we consider the men who presently rule in our country? Do they punish murderers and bank robbers? Or are they promoting anarchy in society? Do we owe them any honor for the law and order that they preserve?

2. At what points might it be appropriate to break the law? Is it possible to break the law and still avoid provoking the magistrate to wrath?

PART 114 ~ THE HIGHWAY OF THE UPRIGHT
Proverbs 16:16

How much better is it to get wisdom than gold! and to get understanding rather than silver!

People will expend blood, sweat, and tears to get something out of life, and most of the time they seem to be motivated by money. The sad fact is that few people value wisdom all that much. Very few young people are seeking wisdom by scanning the pages of the Word of God each day and sitting at the feet of wise masters for hours at a time! It is rare to see young men seeking counsel from the elders in our communities. Why do families rush into all of their money-making activities and household management responsibilities before they spend a few minutes seeking wisdom from the Word of God? Where are their priorities? No matter how much money a society has accumulated, if the people fail to retain wisdom, that society will certainly fall. Wisdom is the principle thing.

Knowledge is also of more value than material wealth. In the hypothetical scenario of the shipwreck where you are faced with the choice between taking a pile of books (the Bible included) or a pile of gold coins off the ship, it would be better to take the books. There is more value to be found in obtaining knowledge, and more dignity graces men gifted with knowledge. Yet knowledge sans wisdom is another perversion, and true knowledge is always formed on a foundation of the fear of God.

Proverbs 16:17

The highway of the upright is to depart from evil: he that keeps his way preserves his soul.

There are only two possible lives to live. Every person who lives and dies on this planet will either live one life or the other. Either he will live his life content in his depraved state, or he will live his life walking away from evil. All of us are born in sin. There is no escaping that reality, but that is only the beginning of a life. Will we continue in sin, or will our lives be characterized by walking away from sin? As the years go by, are we busily peeling off layers of fleshly, sinful tendencies? As others look at the wake of our lives, will they see the dead carcasses of sinful habits lining the path? For the Christian then, life is truly a departure from evil, an abandonment of an old love.

There is no expectation of sinless perfection here, for if there were an age of innocence or a sinless life, there would be no need to depart from evil! Still there are those who, *by faith*, heed the warnings and depart from evil,; and then there are those who do not heed the warnings and fail to flee the "City of Destruction." Fleeing the city in a real sense does save the soul of the upright. When the Bible warns us of the destruction that comes upon the heedless, is it somewhat like

"Cliff Warning" signs on highways in Kansas? Is there no real danger of disaster for those who fail to run away from temptation and evil? As it turns out, those who are the true believers are those who believe the signs. They will always be the runners. They are the ones who heed the warnings, and when they do so they will preserve their own souls by the grace of God.

Family Discussion Question:

1. Where are our priorities as a family? Do we put family worship and family discipleship ahead of our money-making pursuits?

2. As you look at your life, do you see that you are departing from evil? What sins have you mortified lately?

PART 115 ~ ASSOCIATING WITH THE HUMBLE
Proverbs 16:18

Pride goes before destruction, and a haughty spirit before a fall.

Not everything in life is built by pride, but whenever man seeks to build something without giving glory to God, pride takes over. So he proceeds to build his mega corporations, empires, technology, and economies without due regard for God. The years turn into decades, and then to centuries. Human pride only gains more confidence in itself. Man's scientific achievements serve only to embolden him in his proud self-determination. As the years pass, there is no fall, no destruction—only the expansion of man's achievements and his ever-increasing pride. Now he is sure of his own success. He is sure there is no God to enforce such a principle as this one. And, when he least expects it, everything collapses on him. Pride goes before destruction and a haughty spirit before a fall—always.

Having applied this maxim to man's empires and institutions, think how many times we might apply this to ourselves in all of our little experiences in life. Once we have achieved a little success, pride always shows up with party hats for the celebration! Then what happens to our success? A preacher might deliver an excellent sermon on humility. Four people congratulate him on a great message, pride returns, and all is for naught! How many powerful politicians or world-class athletes lose all credibility because of a moral failure? The principle in this verse is confirmed millions of times every day in the lives of billions of people around the world. May God help us to internalize this principle and live our lives by it!

Proverbs 16:19

Better it is to be of an humble spirit with the lowly, than to divide the spoil with the proud.

Generally speaking, humble people are not "cool." As a rule, they are not popular, powerful, or rich. If they are wealthy or powerful, they are usually despised by the masses. But worldly popularity is not worth much, for it is always shallow and fleeting. Proud people think nothing of you, because they think mainly of themselves. They like to play the popularity contests, but who wants to be popular among those who are always proudly turning themselves into gods, not hesitating to put a boot in your face? If you find yourself in the middle of a gathering of proud people who are trying to prove themselves smarter, funnier, better looking, or richer than the next person, excuse yourself from the competition immediately. This is not your game. Instead, go find a group of humble people whom you can learn from. In the end you will find yourself blessed with fruitful, edifying, and enduring relationships.

Family Discussion Questions:

1. Are we a proud family? How does pride manifest itself in our family?

2. Do you ever find yourself pulled into activities or conversations where proud people compete for a position of preeminence? Is it possible to compete over who is the most theologically astute,

or who is the most pious? What could you do to excuse yourself from these groups?

3. How might we do better as a family associating with humble people? What does a humble person look like?

PART 116 ~ LIVING WISELY
Proverbs 16:20

He that handles a matter wisely shall find good: and whoso trusts in the LORD, happy is he.

Life is filled with many interesting challenges and opportunities for the application of true wisdom. Take, for example, the young man who expresses interest in a young woman, but the woman's father finds the suitor a little less than satisfactory. How does the father handle this? Does he shut down the relationship immediately? Will he risk breaking his daughter's heart? Should he take a little time and mentor the young man, or would this be a waste of time and lead to more failed expectations?

This passage recommends two approaches to handling all of life's many complexities, and both are absolutely indispensable. The first requirement is wisdom. As the father approaches the knotty issue of a prospective courtship, every word he speaks must be laced through with wisdom. He must not act out of hypocrisy, imposing a narrow, judgmental standard that he would have never held himself to at the same age. He must understand the feelings of both the young man and the young woman. If he is so hard to approach that his daughter is afraid to tell him her feelings in the matter, then he is already lacking the needed wisdom for making a proper decision. Finally, he must be gentle and peaceable in his approach, such that at the end of the conversation he has not run roughshod over relationships and created rifts that may never be healed. All of these characteristics are contained in the definition of wisdom given in James 3:17.

The second approach that must be employed in the handling of all of life's complicated matters is trust in God. Stepping out into a matter so sensitive and life-determining as a prospective courtship is not much different from Peter climbing out of a boat to walk across the water to meet Jesus. It takes faith! Whether you are raising children, preaching the Gospel, purchasing a house, shepherding young adults through courtships, choosing a church congregation for your family, or just making ordinary decisions everyday—whatever you do, do not attempt any of this without trusting in God. Truly, the just shall live by faith, every day, and every minute of every day.

Proverbs 16:21

The wise in heart shall be called prudent: and the sweetness of the lips increases learning.

A man who makes wise decisions, and says wise things is first wise in heart. That wisdom in his heart exudes from every facet of his being, and others cannot help but see him as a wise man. They will call him "prudent."

But it all begins in the heart. The heart must put first things first. The heart must commit to a life of self-denial and putting others first. The heart must desire the glory of God above all things. The heart must exude humility and grace and love. So you see how all of the onus is on the heart. Where there are no wise hearts, there are no wise men.

The sweetness of the heart will then produce sweetness of the lips. With sweet words come edification, and then people's lives are improved, children are discipled in the ways of God, and homes are filled with joy and peace and fruitful relationships!

Proverbs 16:22

Understanding is a well spring of life unto him that has it: but the instruction of fools is folly.

Why do men persist in rebellion against God? Why do they continually glory in the prospects of spiritual, physical, and eternal death? All those who hate God and His wisdom embrace the paths of death. Sure, they will strive for riches and glory for a limited time on earth, but they know that their inevitable end is death, and they are satisfied with that. Why would they embrace death as their final destiny, except that they have no understanding? They are fools. But to those who are the happy recipients of true understanding will come a bubbling fountain of life. Not only do they seek life, but they will find it—true life, abundant life, even eternal life! What inexpressible happiness awaits those who seek this understanding and find it! But what despair and wretchedness is the lot of those fools who refuse to bend the ear to the instruction of true wisdom!

For related commentary, reference Proverbs 13:14.

Family Discussion Questions:

1. Does our family seek after knowledge? What are the things we do to increase our knowledge and wisdom?

2. Give several examples of matters you have handled wisely. You may also wish to share some examples of matters you did not handle wisely. What was the outcome?

PART 117 ~ THE POWER OF THE TONGUE FOR GOOD

Proverbs 16:23

The heart of the wise teaches his mouth, and adds learning to his lips.

Occasionally, a family member may wake up a little grumpy on a Monday morning. You can tell by the way he greets the others in the morning. His words are only a mirror which reflects the state of his heart. His heart is sour and ungrateful. In the very core of his being, he feels depressed and hopeless in relation to his expectations of the day. Nothing can possibly go right today, he thinks, because God is not good, and God is not in control. Do you see how the heart commitments of a man will affect his attitudes and his words? The heart is the great teacher of the lips.

Proverbs 16:24

Pleasant words are as an honeycomb, sweet to the soul, and health to the bones.

Are you planning to encourage someone in your family or in your church today? Between your two ears you have an instrument which you can use to powerfully encourage your brothers and sisters in Christ. But you must plan your words carefully. The first words out of your mouth in the morning can set the direction for the whole day. Spoken well, your words can be uplifting to the spirit and healthy for the body. In fact, this is the most basic health plan for a family—healthy words. Families who are swamped in a milieu of gossip, bitterness, worry, and depressing, hopeless talk are much more likely to be afflicted by various illnesses. Conversely, the happiest, healthiest families are those who have learned how to speak encouraging, honest, and edifying words to each other in the home.

Family Discussion Questions:

1. What kind of beliefs frames our attitudes? Do we believe in the resurrection of Jesus Christ, and does that have an impact on how we live? When you wake up on Monday morning, what do you believe, and how does that conviction affect your attitude?

2. What kinds of things could we say today that would be an encouragement to each other in our home? Give examples.

PART 118 ~ NATURAL MAN
Proverbs 16:25

There is a way that seems right unto a man, but the end thereof are the ways of death.

Is this some kind of a mistake that Proverbs 14:12 is repeated word for word in this verse? In one important sense, nothing that happens is a mistake. If a scribe in the year 1400 B.C. accidentally repeated a verse in his copy of the Book of Proverbs, and his copy of the text became the accepted Hebrew text for all future Bibles, then we must conclude that God intended this to happen. If there is anything we have learned from the Book of Proverbs thus far, it is that God providentially controls all human events.

When a teacher repeats something for his students, he does so for emphasis. This verse addresses the psychological state of fallen man. He always assumes that he himself is the standard of what is good and right. This is why there are atheists today who act as though they are morally offended by God's destruction of the world by a flood and His destruction of the Canaanites. That atheist may be in favor of homosexuality, abortion, racial quotas, the redistribution of the wealth, and other favorite liberal causes. Of course, he would take great moral offense to God's destruction of homosexuals at Sodom!

But this autonomous attitude also explains why the flesh is so reticent to receive correction. How can the very standard of all that is right and just be questioned? Of course, the problem here is that men are playing the part of God, and this is the very definition of sin and evil.

For related commentary, reference Proverbs 14:12.

Proverbs 16:26

He that labors labors for himself; for his mouth craves it of him.

Where men live with their sin and destructive tendencies, we wonder what keeps society from utterly destroying itself. This verse provides an answer to this puzzle. They work. Even the pagan historian Cicero understood this when he wrote, "People must again learn to work, instead of living on public assistance."

Men, though they are sinners, are still interested in self-preservation. Unless societies have gone the way of the public welfare systems—where the masses are fed by a giant governmental bureaucracy—they still need to work. In the words of the Apostle, "If a man does not work, neither shall he eat" (2 Thess. 3:10). Generally, even the pagans understand this principle, and they work. A man's hunger will drive him to work. As long as men will work, they will not give way to self-destructive habits such as drunkenness, drug addictions, and warring with neighboring tribes. This is the only thing that preserves a society that is not blessed with the sanctifying effects of the Gospel of Christ.

Family Discussion Questions:

1. If men think that they are the very paradigm of morality, how should this affect the way we preach the Gospel to them?

2. If men labor for themselves by nature, why should we labor?

PART 119 ~ DANGEROUS MEN
Proverbs 16:27

An ungodly man digs up evil: and in his lips there is as a burning fire.

Sometimes the Bible refers to these men as sons of Belial. These are typically reprobate men who have heard something of the truth and have hardened themselves against it. They utterly refuse to fear the true and living God, and according to this text, they are dangerous. Even where there is relative peace and quiet, they will find a way to bring mayhem and misery to families, churches, and communities.

One little spark from a vehicle's catalytic converter can touch off a forest fire that destroys fields, homes, hundreds of square miles of beautiful, timbered land. The destructive quality of fire is breathtaking. But what can we say about the tongue? James compares the destructive capacity of the tongue to the fires of hell (James 3:6). These burning flames make for a dangerous servant and a cruel master. If a man who cannot control his tongue is allowed into our communities, he will bring about much destruction. His failure to control his tongue will eventually destroy his marriage and his relationships with his children, friends, and neighbors. His words burn and burn like a fire raging out of control.

Proverbs 16:28

A froward man sows strife: and a whisperer separates chief friends.

The scenario is all too familiar. Several children work for hours on the beach, forming a beautiful, intricately designed castle out of sand. Then some kid charges over and stomps on their work. What kind of a child gets delight out of destroying other peoples' efforts? Obviously, these are destructive, evil people who delight in the misery of others. The Bible calls them "twisted, perverted, and froward." Such behavior is demonic.

Strife and gossip are destructive forces in our homes and churches, and virtually all of us find ourselves giving way to these things from time to time. But there are some who continually employ these forces, wrecking relationships, splitting churches, and generally making a mess out of things. This is what they do. They generate strife and engage in gossip, and they have the remarkable ability to separate even the best of friends! These relationship wreckers have no place in the Christian community of the church. Unless they repent of their sin and repudiate this behavior, they simply cannot continue in the body of the church. At heart they have no intention of edifying or building up the church. Their hearts are held captive by wickedness, and they find their delight in causing misery and destruction.

Proverbs 16:29

A violent man entices his neighbor, and leads him into the way that is not good.

The third dangerous man is the destructive, angry man. Typically, angry people will generate more anger in everyone around them. By his anger, he creates a tension around him that usually spawns more sin. When somebody is angry in the home, he will affect the mood of the home, usually producing more discontentment, more complaining, more unkind words, and more bitterness and resentment. In short, the violent, angry man who tries to get his own way by brute force will inevitably destroy his relationships and undermine his own leadership. He may try to get things done by brute force and tyrannical means, but in the end he will find that his work yielded more destruction than positive good. If his sons or employees emulate his abusive ways, they will only multiply the carnage, adding to the man's legacy of broken families and businesses.

Proverbs 16:30

He shuts his eyes to devise froward things: moving his lips he brings evil to pass.

Once when conducting a pastoral visit in a home, I noticed that the family had a pet dog that was confined to the kitchen/dining area. He was not allowed on the carpet in the living room. But as we were visiting that evening, I noticed that the dog placed his paws over his eyes and elbowed his way onto the carpet! Apparently, the dog had convinced himself that because he could not see what he was doing, he could be innocent of the guilt of his action. Are men any different when they devise ways to break the laws of God, convincing themselves at the same time that they will not be held liable by Almighty God for what they are doing? They pretend either that God does not exist, or that they are not really doing what they are doing. Somehow, they are able to hide themselves from the reality of their own sinful actions. For a time, they block out the reality of judgment, the all-seeing eye of God, and the truly evil nature of their actions.

It is also very easy for him to commit these evil actions. It really takes very little effort. By simply moving his lips for two or three seconds, heinous blasphemy against God pours forth, lies work their deceit, and more relationships die.

Family Discussion Questions:

1. What should we do with people who sow strife and separate good friends? Do we associate with them? What if we should find them in our church communities?

2. Are there certain times in our family where sins like complaining, discontentment, arguing, and bitterness seem to multiply? How does this happen?

3. How does sinful anger manifest itself in violence and destruction? Do we see this kind of thing in our own home?

PART 120 ~ TRUE GREATNESS
Proverbs 16:31

The hoary [gray] head is a crown of glory if it be found in the way of righteousness.

The elderly are often ignored and even despised by the younger crowd in this day and age. Those who are not shuffled away into their own little retreat centers or their own churches find it exceedingly hard to fit in with the younger generation. With a constantly changing culture and updated technology, these old folks are seen out of date, unimportant, or just in the way.

All of this betrays the utter foolishness of modern society. For there is a great deal of technical knowledge in our day, yet we have precious little *real* wisdom. Only age and experience in the way of righteousness could ever produce a reservoir of wisdom with which a community might prosper.

The implications are obvious. We must consider our gray-haired men and women with honor and great esteem. These are the ones who have gone before us; they have waged a thousand battles against the world and the flesh, and they have established a heritage on which we will stand. How might we express this respect? The Mosaic law calls us to rise up when in the presence of an elderly man or woman. This means that we must take note of them when in their presence and render them some form of special honor beyond that which we might ordinarily show others.

Proverbs 16:32

He that is slow to anger is better than the mighty; and he that rules his spirit than he that takes a city.

Great men are often known for their military conquests or feats of incredible physical strength. For their amazing accomplishments, they may even win a mention in the *Guinness Book of World Records.* But there are some things that are even more difficult, more strenuous, and more important to God than the ability to lift a 6,000 pound car over your head. Among the most impressive qualities of all is the ability to control your emotions. Taking a city in a military conquest is a formidable task. You will have to fight every inch of the way, scale the walls in the face of torrents of fire power, and killing a hundred enemies in your path. But getting a hand on your emotions, or cooling off your anger before you say something unwise or hurtful, can be overwhelmingly difficult. Emotions are not sinful. They are powerful things for good or for evil. But to carefully and wisely employ your emotions in service to the glory of God and the advancement of Christ's kingdom is a superhuman task.

Family Discussion Questions:

1. Does our family treat the elderly with the kind of respect they deserve? In our culture, what would be some good ways by which we might show more honor to our elderly?

2. In what situations might it be very difficult to control your emotions? Which emotions do we have the most difficulty controlling?

PART 121 ~ THE ULTIMATE CAUSE
Proverbs 16:33

The lot is cast into the lap; but the whole disposing thereof is of the LORD.

From the most highly educated men on the earth, and the greatest philosophers that the humanists have ever produced, we learn that there are only two explanations for what will happen in the future: either things are predetermined, or they are not determined at all. Either there is a force in the universe that will certainly effect some certain end, or everything is chaos and there is no purpose or order to the universe. Now, the problem with an indeterminate universe is that all human action becomes ultimately purposeless and amoral. If we are all just pinballs bouncing around in a gigantic machine, then we certainly can't be held responsible for our actions, and all of our actions are superbly unimportant.

On the other hand, the problem with a determinate universe is that we can hardly be held responsible for our actions. If some powerful force is determining every action we take, whether we rob a bank or help an elderly lady across the street, then how can we be held responsible for our decisions? Thus you can see why the greatest philosophers that have ever lived cannot explain the universe in such a way that moral responsibility and purpose are retained.

But even though the wisest men have failed in their attempts to answer these ultimate questions, it is incumbent on Christians to provide an answer. What determines whether I will produce a '6' or a '12' when I roll the dice? Or does nothing determine it? If it is a matter of the force of my fingers, the air currents in the room, and the weight distribution of the dice, we must still ask whether there is any other ultimate force or cause that produced the air currents, the force of the roll, and the weight of the dice, assuring that I would roll a six or a twelve at this moment. What determines what will happen? Do we live in an indeterminate, by chance universe, or do we live in a determinate universe? This verse gives a clear answer. It is a determinate universe of sorts. God has predetermined whether you will roll a six or a twelve! He knows the outcome before you roll the dice because He causes it. Yet, the Bible does not present God as an impassive force at all. When God predetermines what will happen in the future, He does so as a personal God Who can work His plan through the free actions of men while retaining their moral responsibility. Obviously, this is something that the rest of us cannot do. We cannot assure that we will roll a six, or that some men will rob a bank on Monday, or that others will crucify the Lord of glory on Friday, for that matter. But then again we are not able to create universes out of nothing either.

God controls the outcome of everything, right down to the rolling of the dice in hundreds of gambling houses and casinos. From the significant human events, like the election of a president, to every insignificant effect that plays into the more important occurrences, God controls it all. This is the indisputable lesson of Scripture—and it constitutes the most basic proposition of a biblical theory of reality, not to mention the biblical definition of God.

Family Discussion Question:

1. If God controls everything, down to the outcome of a toss of the dice, how does this affect the way you play games, work, and live your life?

PART 122 ~ HEALTHY HOUSEHOLD ECONOMIES
Proverbs 17:1

Better is a dry morsel, and quietness therewith, than an house full of sacrifice with strife.

In the Old Testament era, the Jews would partake of part of what was sacrificed on the altar to God. Of course, the sacrifice was usually meat, such as beef or mutton. Therefore, a household of sacrifice was a home blessed with a great deal of meat taken from the sacrifices. These meat-stuffed homes enjoyed more material wealth than the homes whose cupboards resembled Old Mother Hubbard's. For most people, a dinner of meat beats a crust of bread every day!

But what is it that really provides joy and contentment in a home? Is it wealth? Is it steaks on the barbecue, chocolate cream pies, or an indoor swimming pool? No, peace is essential for happy homes. The kingdom of God is righteousness, peace, and joy in the Holy Spirit (Rom. 14).

Sometimes material wealth adds to the contention in the home, especially when people value money over relationships. How often do marriages break up over disagreements concerning finances? Of course, this is pure foolishness. It is a failure in priorities. It is a refusal to value the things that God values such as peace and biblical conflict resolution. If necessary, we must be willing to sacrifice our wealth, our fast-paced lives, and our materialistic pursuits for the sake of peace and unity within the home. May God give us homes where men will confess their sins to their wives, where forgiveness flows all the time, where humility reigns, and where peace prevails!

Proverbs 17:2

A wise servant shall have rule over a son that causes shame, and shall have part of the inheritance among the brethren.

Generally, a biblical economy is a household economy. Large, centralized corporate systems are relatively new phenomena in the history of the world, and as they have come to dominate in the economy, they have almost completely eliminated household-based economies. The goal of this new economic system was to produce a centralized economy easily controlled and regulated by government. The word "economics" comes from the Greek *oikonomia*, which is translated "the vision of the family." The basic economic unit is the family. Although large corporations pretend to provide security and loyalty to their employees, and centralized governments appear to "love" the elderly for whom they provide "social security," in actuality they are only cruel, power-oriented benefactors (Luke 22:25–26).

The household economy is based in relationships and long-term loyalty, eventually producing something called "inheritance." Instead of consuming their children's inheritance as many "retired" people do in our present day, good men are interested in building their family's economic well-being by passing an inheritance on to future generations.

A household economy typically includes sons or daughters, as well as a couple of hired employees or apprentices. Because some young men are not prepared to run their own household economies, they should seek apprenticeships with other men who operate their own family economic ventures. Should the apprentice submit himself to the counsel and teaching of the older man, he will learn the wisdom and the skills provided by the mentorship. Sadly, there are some young sons whose hearts are so full of pride and dishonor for their fathers that they prove themselves as unfaithful, foolish, and highly unproductive sons. This can be more prevalent among wealthy families—where wealth has created pride, slothfulness, and deficiency of character in the children. So, if a father mentors a young apprentice in his business and finds the apprentice far more productive and willing to learn than his own son, to whom do you think he would be more likely to turn over his household business? In a day when honor of parents is practically negligible, and where wealth has corrupted the character of an entire generation, we can see this proverb particularly and painfully relevant!

Proverbs 17:3

The refining pot is for silver, and the furnace for gold: but the LORD tries the hearts.

Tests, trials, and tribulations are all part of life, because God intended it to be so! Always, He is testing us for our faith and our love. Will we grow embittered against Him, or will we turn to Him for deliverance in this trial or that? Some hearts will harden and some will soften. The same fire of tribulation that melts one heart will harden another heart into steel. Trials only betray what lies underneath.

When we first begin to walk with the Lord, our faith is weak and fledgling. Faith starts out as a tender plant. But, sustained by the grace of God and the watering of the Word, that little plant flourishes under the intense sun of tribulation. This is how we interpret the challenges and difficulties of life. Some view their hard times as bad luck. But when you stub your toe, lose your wallet, or fail in a business, each one of these trying circumstances is an intentional event in your life. They are there to test you. You will either see them as bad luck in a causeless universe, the malevolent designs of an angry God, or the wise, loving, shepherding of a kind Father. Did you stub your toe because God wanted to do you in, or is God teaching you something at that moment? Your interpretation of the things that happen to you is based on what you believe about God and your relationship with Him. Everything that happens to you will test these beliefs.

Family Discussion Questions:

1. Does covetousness or wealth make us discontent and contentious? Is there peace in our home? How might our home be more peaceful?

2. How might we avoid spoiling our sons? Is wealth corrupting our children?

3. How do you react in trials? Do they draw you closer to God, or distance you from Him?

PART 123 ~ REAL SCOUNDRELS
Proverbs 17:4

A wicked doer gives heed to false lips; and a liar gives EAR to a naughty tongue.

Sitting in the lunch room at work, a Christian employee observes carefully as some fellow begins spouting off filthy jokes, slander, flagrant exaggeration, and assorted blasphemous phrases. He is forward and aggressive—a leader of sorts. Some are drawn to his wicked speech while others are repulsed by it. Why are some attracted to this wicked speech? Their hearts are not right with God. They themselves are living a wicked lifestyle, and the words they hear serve as an apologetic for the life they live. Fundamentally, anyone who lives a godless, fornicating, drunken lifestyle is living one big lie. He believes the fatal falsehood that he has no moral accountability to the God Who created him. If some loud nutcase in the workplace can support him in this belief, he'll gladly take his place in the audience to hear the profane drivel pouring out of the man's lips.

Proverbs 17:5

Whoso mocks the poor reproaches his Maker: and he that is glad at calamities shall not be unpunished.

Both Old and New Testaments are equally firm on this matter of the treatment of the poor. How a society deals with its poor will indicate how much the Christian faith has truly penetrated those cultures. We are warned not to despise the poor, or to assume, as did Job's comforters, that it was the man's sin that merited his miserable condition. But why is a man in an impoverished condition? There is only one absolutely and certainly true answer to that question: God ordained it. Therefore, to mock the poor is equivalent to mocking God Himself. Moreover, it is not a man's financial condition that establishes his worth or his dignity. First and foremost, any man made in the image of God is worthy of respect. Then, it is a man's character, relationships, and accomplishments that form his reputation—and none of these have a direct connection with his net worth. Also, what can we say about the reasonably wealthy man who gave every dime he had to charitable institutions and ministry efforts, willingly embracing poverty in order that others might prosper?

What kind of person would mock a poor man, except one who assumes the worst of him? "He's only getting what he deserves" is the assumption. But what exactly do the rest of us deserve? How is our sin, idolatry, pride, and lust any different from the next person's? Perhaps our lust for pleasure and materials did not take us all the way to drug addiction and abject poverty as it did for some poor fellow living in the slums, but even that is a matter of the protective grace of God.

We never have the right to delight in the sufferings of others, even at that moment in which we might witness our most committed enemies being run over by a truck. David was the prime example of the truly gracious man when he wept over the death of his deadly enemy, King Saul (2 Sam. 1). While it may be appropriate to rejoice in the just acts of God in history, be careful. Should *we* escape any calamity or judgment at the hands of the Judge of the universe, it is all grace—nothing but grace! If, however, some other person fails to escape, none of his suffering comes as a consequence of his sins against us. Rather, every ounce of judgment comes as just punishment for his sins against an infinitely holy and righteous God. To claim some part of the judgment for our own vengeance is to attempt to steal from the glory of God and His right to establish the absolute standard of justice.

Family Discussion Questions:

1. What is our reaction when we find ourselves in the company of a liar or a foul-mouthed character? How should we react?

2. Why is it inappropriate to delight in the sufferings of others, even of your enemies?

3. What is our perspective of the poor in our midst? Do we try to humbly serve them as we can, or do we assume the worst of them?

PART 124 ~ HONORABLE MEN AND FOOLS
Proverbs 17:6

Children's children are the crown of old men; and the glory of children are their fathers.

If you read through the Scriptures, you will find a good many crowns. The woman is the crown of the man, fathers are the crown of children, and grandchildren are the crown of grandfathers. From 1 Corinthians 11:5ff we learn that the man is the glory of God, and the woman is the glory of the man. As a crown announces to all the honor due to the one who wears it, so the mere existence of a man announces to the world the honor and glory due to God Who created him.

Now we may better understand the verse at hand. When somebody snaps a picture of a grandfather surrounded by his five children and thirty-two grandchildren at a family reunion, it makes for quite an impressive picture! All of these grandchildren and children serve as a sort of crown, presenting the grandfather as a man who is worthy of great honor. None of them would be there had it not been for this man.

Yet the converse is true as well—"The glory of children are their fathers." What renders honor and value to a child is the love of a father! The father/child relationship is fundamental to a child's sense of well-being and dignity. A father's love is one-thousand times more important than getting into a good college or inheriting ten million dollars from a distant relative. But more than this, a well-respected father gives the son and daughter a certain credibility as well. If a father is serving time in prison for drug trafficking, his reputation will not provide much credibility to his children.

This is a powerful verse indeed as it speaks to the precious value of our relationships and our heritage.

Proverbs 17:7

Excellent speech is not fitting for a fool: much less do lying lips a prince.

In January of 2010 a Navy commander was stripped of her command of the *U.S.S. Cowpens* because of her habitual use of foul language with her subordinates. Apparently, even the decadent, humanist systems of the day still maintain some regard for "excellent speech" and an honorable decorum. Princes, army generals, and political leaders may get away with lies and dishonoring language for a little while, but they are only undermining themselves and the organizations they pretend to lead when they give way to these things. When the Vice President of the United States used some of the most foul language imaginable at the signing of the socialist health care bill of 2010, it was only another indication that the empire was in its final death throes.

Fools are incapable of excellent speech. They may resort to reading from a teleprompter as many leaders do today, and if they are careful not to intersperse their own thoughts in their speech, they may come across as someone better than a fool. But should they vent their own thought in an honest moment, the truth will show their character. They are fools, and soon everyone will know it.

Family Discussion Questions:

1. What does it mean when the Bible speaks of grandchildren as the crown of a grandfather? What is meant by the term "crown"?

2. What can fathers do to honor their children?

3. How often do you hear princes and politicians tell lies? What does this do to the integrity of the political systems over us?

PART 125 ~ GIFTS AND FRIENDSHIPS
Proverbs 17:8

A gift is as a precious stone in the eyes of him that has it: whithersoever it turns, it prospers.

A gift is a beautiful thing. Have you ever received a gift? No matter how insignificant, a gift is more precious than anything you might purchase for yourself. It is one thing for you to purchase an apple at the farmer's market for your own consumption: The purchase is insignificant. But should a poor widow in the church give you an apple as a gift, it would be hard to forget such a meager, yet significant act of love! A gift is far more meaningful than the material enrichment of the one who receives it.

Gifts are persuasive. Gifts will solidify relationships. Gifts are symbols of love, and it is hard for the receiver to interpret them any other way. Of course, wicked people use gifts to pervert justice and gain illegitimate favor. They have ulterior motives in their gift-giving. But with our brothers and sisters, any way you look at the gift, it communicates friendship and love.

Proverbs 17:9

He that covers a transgression seeks love; but he that repeats a matter separates very [close] friends.

Relationships are tenuous things, especially in our present day. Most people would rather not have close relationships with others because those relationships seem to bring about disappointment, offense, and broken friendships. Therefore, the people of the world do what they can to insulate themselves from the pain by separating themselves from others. They constantly move from city to city and from church to church to get lost in the crowd. Loneliness characterizes modern life.

But true biblical community returns to human society when the content of this verse becomes the fabric of our lives. The only way to cultivate loving, fruitful relationships is to cover transgressions—to forget about other people's sins—constantly. It is to live with an "abiding amnesia" in relation to the sins of others. This is the only way for relationships to prosper and to keep them from being choked by bitterness and anger. Of course, if a man is committing gross crimes, he should be turned over to the police and the civil courts, who must adjudicate the matter according to the justice of God's laws. But when fathers and elders lovingly confront their children or other church members concerning sin, it is important that they quickly "burn the files" in their minds, so they themselves are not taken by the sin of bitterness.

The second way in which biblical community is fostered in our family and church life is by the careful bridling of the tongue. Any time you speak about someone else outside of his presence is akin to opening his underwear drawer. Now you are discussing their personal affairs, and you must be extremely careful with how you proceed. Perhaps it would be better just to shut the drawer and move on. If there is a sin that must be dealt with in your friend's life, what profit is there draging the sin around for everybody else to see it? How is this going to solve the problem? To gossip about somebody else's faults only creates rifts and builds walls. And it does little or nothing to lead the sinning brother to repentance. Those who tolerate gossip usually begin to configure the brother as someone hardened in his sin. They form an inaccurate caricature of him, one that is usually far worse than what he is in reality. Do you see how unedifying and destructive gossip can be in our fellowships?

Family Discussion Questions:

1. What kind of power does a gift exert on those who receive it?

2. Are we as a family generous in our gift giving? How can we be better at giving gifts?

3. How effective are we at forgetting the sins of others? Do we "burn the files" in our minds, or do we keep records of wrongs?

4. Is it appropriate to talk about others behind their backs? How do people feel when you open their underwear drawers?

PART 126 ~ REBELS AND FOOLS
Proverbs 17:10

A reproof enters more into a wise man than an hundred stripes into a fool.

This is another wonderful illustration of the foolish scoffer, the teenage rebel who is so characterized by scoffing that he cannot be corrected. Biblically, nobody should ever receive more than forty stripes. This means that if you have a scoffer on your hands, no amount of beating will ever change the heart of that man. He is a fool, and he simply cannot be taught wisdom. May God help all of us, that we may never be so foolish that we cannot receive wisdom!

Please note that these warnings concerning foolish scoffing are dispersed throughout the Book of Proverbs just in case our children might at any point be falling into this trap. If you have a persistent scoffer on your hands, whatever you are teaching during these times in the Word is just a waste of time.

Proverbs 17:11

An evil man seeks only rebellion: therefore a cruel messenger shall be sent against him.

Sadly, there are some who fit the category of a "total rebel," and these men are described by the holy law of God in Deuteronomy 21:18–21 and Matthew 15:4 as the rebellious son who gets drunk, strikes his mother or father, and curses at them. At the point where a man casts off all honor of father and mother, he becomes unmanageable by family, church, and state. If he will not honor his own father, of course he will not honor the civil magistrate. Inevitably, these men will go on to plunder, rape, and kill others. Follow the careers of most criminals, and you will note that they almost always begin with an unrestrained rebellion against their mothers and fathers. It would have been better had the magistrate obeyed Deuteronomy 21. How many murders might have been prevented, and how much more stability would society enjoy, if men would respect God's laws?

Yet most of the time the civil magistrate is not interested in containing rebellious sons until the society degrades into substantial anarchy. So whether the young man is killed in a gunfight with a police officer or at the hands of some rival gang, his rebellion will surely destroy him. There is always sufficient cruelty to meet whatever cruelty he has mustered in his rebellion. Those who live by the sword die by the sword (Matt. 26:52).

Proverbs 17:12

Let a bear robbed of her whelps [cubs] meet a man, rather than a fool in his folly.

How would you like to wander into the path of a mother bear just a few seconds after someone had snatched her cubs and driven away with them? It would be hard to come up with a more dreadful, frightening circumstance! But here the wise sage presents an even worse possible scenario—you enter into a business relationship with a fool. Or you begin to spend time with a cadre of drunkards on the weekends. Or you get tangled up in an online relationship with a foolish young man or woman on the Internet. (By the way, with 12% of young men pathologically addicted to computer games, you will most certainly be likely to meet some fools in this medium.) You should really prefer a run-in with the mother bear than to be taken by a fool. The lesson here is clear: stay far away from fools! These folks may be winsome and persuasive. They may be very sure of themselves, their success at computer games, and their ability to ignore God in their philosophy classrooms. But do not be taken by them! Just as a mother bear can gnaw on your head and scrape your skin off, these people will take your soul apart and destroy your reputation and your life.

Family Discussion Questions:

1. Is discipline effective for a fool? Why or why not?

2. What happens to teenage rebels who harden themselves in their rebellion?

3. What kind of relationship might you want to maintain with a fool? Would you ever speak to him? Would you have him over for dinner? Would you enter into a business partnership with him?

PART 127 ~ REWARDING EVIL
Proverbs 17:13, 15

Whoso rewards evil for good, evil shall not depart from his house.
He that justifies the wicked, and he that condemns the just, even they
both are abomination to the LORD.

What a frightening warning to those who insist on persecuting the righteous! This particularly applies to those who have access to power. According to Romans 13 the civil magistrate is duty-bound to reward the good and punish what is evil; and good and evil may only be defined by the righteous standard of God's law. Therefore, when governments reward homosexuals and prosecute those who say something that is in opposition to homosexual behavior, we would conclude, by the clear dictates of God's laws, that these legislators or judges will suffer the curse of God upon them and their families. This curse may also extend to all those whom they represent. In the case of the Sodomites, who themselves tolerated evil and persecuted the righteous, the entire city-state felt the brunt of God's judgment.

There is a God in the heavens, and He will certainly bring justice where there is injustice. It is only for us to stand and defend the righteous laws of God, love our neighbor as ourselves, and live peaceably with all men. Every government subsidy of abortion, every public school that promotes homosexuality, every economic policy that breaks down the integrity of the family, and every preacher of God's Word arrested by the magistrates will not go unnoticed by the Magistrate of Heaven! Those in positions of power that oppose righteousness will only bring the destruction they wrought back down on their own heads. They only construct monuments to their own ignominy. They destroy the social systems they pretend to lead.

Proverbs 17:14

The beginning of strife is like the releasing of water: therefore stop contention before a quarrel starts.

Here is the secret to maintaining peace in the family. The best point to stop a fight is at the beginning because each new word uttered in an argument serves only to intensify the anger and resistance on both sides. How much easier would it be if you could patch the dam break when it is nothing more than a small stream of water, instead of waiting until it turns into a raging torrent?

We need to be "on our game" when it comes to addressing small sources of irritation and disagreement in our family life.

Always be prepared to conciliate, quickly confess your own sin in a conflict, provide a soft answer, or encourage a brother or sister to remain humble. Listen for raised voices, exaggerated accusations, or impatient irritation, and be ready to patch the cracks in the dam right away.

Proverbs 17:15

He that justifies the wicked, and he that condemns the just, even they both are abominations to the LORD.

For related commentary, reference Proverbs 17:13.

Proverbs 17:16

Wherefore is there a price in the hand of a fool to get wisdom, seeing he has no heart to it?

Occasionally you will find a fool who appears to be seeking wisdom. He might even pay $40,000 to attend Harvard University each year, while he participates in drunken fraternity parties or takes part in the atheist club on campus. If the fool has said in his heart, "There is no God," the university man who argues against God's existence has no heart for wisdom. The end result of his studies and his work will be the breaking down of institutions, the destruction of science, and the collapse of a civilization.

Family Discussion Questions:

1. What happens to legislators who vote for hate-crime laws in order to prosecute pastors who preach against homosexuality?

2. When is the best time to stop an argument or prevent a church split?

3. Why do fools appear to seek after wisdom when they really have no heart for it?

PART 128 ~ FRIENDSHIP
Proverbs 17:17

A friend loves at all times, and a brother is born for adversity.

In this first part of the 21st century, there are five times more people living alone as there were nearly one hundred years ago. It is doubtful that the world has ever been so lonely as it is today, with all of its big cities, busy schedules, materialism, anonymous lives, and transience. People hardly stay in the same place for more than a couple years at a time. Just visit a hospital Intensive Care Unit in a metropolis and count the family or friends sitting in the waiting rooms; then you will understand the severe isolation that defines our world. Over six or seven generations, we have been carefully trained by our social systems to live without friendship. If we had a childhood friend, or friends in the workplace, or friends in a church, we learned to move away from those friendships regularly in our lives. Friendship is almost dead in our world.

But not so in God's world! According to this text, a true friend loves through thick and thin, through bad times and good times. However, challenges often come within friendships when we move to a new town or church that is away from friends. It is quite possible that the friends we have moved away from will cease to be our friends, and we may be hesitant to create close friendships again because we expect those friendships to fail as well. This is the trajectory of many friendships. But against all this comes the biblical definition of friendship. A true friend loves at all times, and a true brother will stick by you through adversity. Of course, it is true that we cannot be friends with everyone we know, and the Bible is careful not to prescribe that. Some people are able to cultivate more friendships than others, but the more acquaintances you make, the harder it can be to establish true friendships. Still, the principle of the matter stands—be a friend. Learn true friendship. Find a friend and stick with him all the way to the end.

Proverbs 17:18

A man void of understanding strikes hands, and becomes surety in the presence of his friend.

Although much of the "modern" world relies upon debt, rentals, and long-term contractual arrangements, these economic systems are always fraught with peril. The final chapter of the American empire will forever testify to the truth of these wise sayings! Our banking systems were based on nothing but debt. They played cards with the devil and raised the odds a thousand times! They borrowed trillions of dollars, and then they borrowed on the IOUs! Encouraged by the banks, people borrowed money and bought houses in their attempts to get rich in what they hoped would be a perpetually inflating real-estate market. Then the banks turned the mortgages into play money, and investors bought the play money (or derivatives) through investment and insurance companies with money from those who consumed less than they produced. But in the end, everybody borrowed more than they produced until there was plenty of money, and as the poet Kipling said,

> *"...there was nothing that money could buy,*
> *and the gods of the copybook headings said,*
> *'If you don't work you die!'"*[1]

Lending to a stranger is one thing, but this particular proverb speaks to the matter of lending to a friend or even renting a home to a friend. What happens if your friend finds he is unable to keep the contract or fails to uphold his side of the bargain, due to a loss of a job or some other circumstance? You would find it far better to give the home to your friend and thereby retain that friendship than to risk losing your friendship over the rental. You could lend the property to your friend free of charge, but this can also be risky. Should he return the property to you in worse condition, this also might threaten to erode the integrity of your friendship.

---

1 Kipling, Rudyard, "The Gods of the Copybook Headings"

Because we have wandered so far from a biblical economic system, these ideas are quite foreign to us. But they provide good, solid wisdom. What we find in Scripture is the priority of friendship. Our friends are precious, and relationships always trump economics.

For related commentary, reference Proverbs 6:5 and Proverbs 11:15.

Family Discussion Questions:

1. What is the definition of a friend? Are we good friends in our family, and do we have anybody we could call a true friend?

2. Is it wise to lend money or rent your house out to a friend? What might be a better way to help out your friend?

PART 129 ~ PRIDE AND STRIFE
Proverbs 17:19

He loves transgression that loves strife: and he that exalts his gate seeks destruction.

Some people get a thrill out of launching an incendiary comment into a conversation, and others are more than happy to return another tirade of words, loaded with more angry, less-than-edifying sentiments. Somebody lights the fire, and somebody else throws gasoline on it. This happens in conversations between husbands and wives in the kitchen, in many academic debates, and within the endless Internet blogs and comment strings. All of these exchanges are unedifying because there is no real interest in seeing a brother edified. Winning arguments is everything for these people, but nobody is really edified or persuaded in the process. They glory in the fight, the volcanic emotions, and their own performance in the debate. The root of this contentious spirit is ultimately pride, and that is what is addressed in the second half of the verse.

The thirst for power becomes intoxicating for some people, and when this quest for power becomes endemic throughout entire societies, the results are catastrophic. Power centralizes and the masses are enslaved. This has certainly been the legacy of modern countries since the turn of the 20th century. In fact, governments are five to ten times more powerful than they were one-hundred years ago. The thirst for more power draws both the socialist democrats and the capitalist republicans with equal force. Each attempts to collect more power to further its own interests. But it is always more power that they seek. Inevitably, this power-chase and the centralization of power and money effect a breakdown of morality, a corruption of the nuclear family, and the eventual collapse of healthy economies.

Proverbs 17:20

He that has a froward heart finds no good: and he that has a perverse tongue falls into mischief.

If the heart is the boat motor and the tongue is the rudder, then the heart and the tongue together will take the boat wherever it is going to go. Will the boat chug up the river or meander down a tributary and then drop over a waterfall? It will be the motor and the rudder that will determine its course.

This being the case, you can see how important it is for parents to train the heart and the tongue by patient teaching in the Word. And if a "teenager" be cursed with a rebellious heart and an uncontrolled tongue, you know the choices that young person makes may very well destroy his or her life.

Proverbs 17:21

He that begets a fool does it to his sorrow: and the father of a fool has no joy.

Within the same family, you can often find one son who is honorable, teachable, and God-fearing, and another son who turns out to be a rebellious, drunken fool. Certainly we find these sorts of families in Scripture, from Cain and Abel to Absalom and Solomon. How does one explain this strange occurrence? There is, of course, the matter of training a child in the way he should go. But there is also the sovereign hand of God working, for we read in Scripture that before Jacob and Esau were capable of good and evil, God preferred one over the other (Rom. 9:10ff). We find that human responsibility and God's sovereignty are *both* elements in the development of a child's character.

This verse merely describes the curse upon a family when a son turns out to be a fool. Suppose a child who is playing the fool should hear this verse read in family devotions. Do you think that he might take fair warning from such a passage and think to himself, "Would to God that I turn from the way of rebellion! Why should I bring shame down upon my poor father?" Or is the fool so bound in his foolishness and self-centeredness that such notions are meaningless to him?

Proverbs 17:22

A merry heart does good like a medicine: but a broken spirit dries the bones.

There are 100,000 theories running around about what it takes to live a long and healthy life. Because of the millions of possible interactions between various causes and effects, it is utterly impossible to determine which snake oil, diet, or lifestyle choice could produce the highest probabilities for good health. Generally, smoking is unhealthy, but some smokers live into their 100s. What were the things they did that counteracted the negative effects of smoking? Again, there is no certain way to find these things out. It is just too difficult to control lifelong experiments on human beings. Therefore, we are left with debates over every American Medical Association hypothesis, alternative health plan, and old wives' tale that issues from the experts of the hour. We find that some approaches to diet and bodily maintenance may work better for some people than for others. Yet even then we cannot draw these conclusions with very much confidence. There will always be a measure of guesswork.

Nevertheless, there are some universal principles related to health that come to us by divine wisdom, and they ought to overshadow all of the billions of man-made theories that proliferate everywhere. Verse 22 provides one of these principles.

Family Discussion Questions:

1. Do you enjoy arguing and debating with others? At what point does a healthy discussion or debate turn into strife?

2. Are we a proud family, interested only in our own power and success? How might we mitigate this kind of pride?

3. Why is the rebel content to see his parents utterly devastated and ruined by his rebellion?

4. What is God's theory on physical health and well-being?

PART 130 ~ BRIBES AND WISE LEADERSHIP
Proverbs 17:23

A wicked man takes a gift out of the bosom to pervert the ways of judgment.

When half of the economy is controlled by power brokers in Washington D.C., there is no hope for honest government. Absolute power corrupts absolutely. So it should be no surprise that the top donors to George W. Bush's presidential campaign of 2004 were the same as the top donors to the Barrack Obama presidential campaign of 2008. They were, of course, Wall Street financial institutions. The reason why these organizations provided so much money to these campaigns became clear in the latter half of 2008, when George W. Bush turned over $800 billion in taxpayer monies to rescue these same banks and financial institutions during the Great Recession! The institutional fraud that constitutes modern government is staggering. Sadly, it has become a way of life for this country, and it is hard to find one in a hundred people who care about it enough to support somebody who does not use his political position in this way.

But know that every single campaign donation that results in government funding of welfare, special interests, or budget items favoring one state over another, will only serve to pervert justice and undermine the integrity of a nation. If a particular vote places a military installation in one state instead of some other state, the congressman representing the state receiving the economic benefit should exempt himself from the debate and the vote. Not one dime given to his campaign should have anything to do with the projects funded in the state budgets, whether they be education, welfare, road construction, or military-related projects.

When at least 60% of a nation's economy is controlled by elected governments made up of sinful men, the legislatures devolve into a confused scheme of redistributing wealth—and everybody feels the need to grab their "fair share." The few productive people left are subjected to ever increasing levels of taxation to fund this fraudulent free-for-all. This is how the largest nations the world has ever seen will come to their end. Violating the principles of God's Word always leads to judgment.

Proverbs 17:24

Wisdom is before him that has understanding; but the eyes of a fool are in the ends of the earth.

Wisdom is easily accessible to the person who is already blessed with an understanding spirit. Speaking of the basic Gospel, Paul speaks of the word accessible to you "even in your mouth and in your heart." But this can only be said for that person whose heart has already been awakened by the Spirit of God (1 Cor. 2:9–14). Meanwhile, the eyes of the fool search high and low for wisdom. He reads 100,000 books, changes his religion a hundred times in his life, and secures five doctorate degrees. But it is all for nothing, for in him is not to be found the spirit of understanding.

Proverbs 17:25

A foolish son is a grief to his father, and bitterness to her that bore him.

What is impressed here upon the foolish son is the curse he has become to his own father and mother. How heart wrenching it is to see a good mother's life turned to unrelenting, teeth-grinding bitterness! This is the woman who went through unspeakable pain as she birthed her son, not to mention the many years of nursing, physical attention, and care. She gave of her own life, emotions, and energy to raise this child. But now the young man has become a source of grief and a curse to his parents. Of all the wretched effects of sin in the world, this sad circumstance may be the most horrible and miserable.

For related commentary, reference Proverbs 17:21.

Proverbs 17:26

Also to punish the just is not good, nor to strike princes for equity.

The wise man is particularly passionate about the matters of justice in the civil sphere, evidenced by the string of sage lessons contained in verses 13, 15, and 23. The practice of "striking" hands involves a secret agreement, usually based upon a bribe. Any compromise on justice or equitable treatment under the law only serves to break apart civil governments, whether the system of government is monarchy or democracy. Interestingly, the Bible has little to say about the form of government. Either democracies or monarchies can be corrupted either by failing to prosecute crimes according to the just requirements of God's law, or by bribing and campaign donations that result in the unjust confiscation of property and redistribution of wealth.

Proverbs 17:27

He that has knowledge spares his words: and a man of understanding is of an excellent spirit.

Here we are given a picture of a very rare person indeed. This is a man who carefully measures every word he speaks. But more than this, he is not easily discouraged. His indomitable resilience in spirit is encouraging to those whom he leads in his family or church. He does not over-react to criticism, but he will humbly receive wise counsel and reasonable correction. He never gives way to angry rants or vindictive actions. It is this spirit to which others are drawn, and this is fundamental to leadership. While some, like Reuben, are as "unstable as water," this man may be counted on for his excellence of spirit in the midst of confusion, war, death, and persecutions. He is always hopeful, always courageous, and always faithful to his friends.

Proverbs 17:28

Even a fool, when he holds his peace, is counted wise: and he that shuts his lips is esteemed a man of understanding.

In a less charitable frame of mind, somebody once quipped, "It is better to keep your mouth shut and be thought a fool than to open it and remove all doubt." Of course, this verse deals with the perceptions of others. It explains why some fools are still respected, and that goes for a good many atheists and idolatrous materialists. Many do not wear their godlessness and foolishness on their sleeves. Thus, by keeping all that foolishness clapped up tightly inside, they retain a measure of respect and success in business and civil government.

Family Discussion Questions:

1. What happens when a nation relies on bribes and forcible redistribution of wealth?

2. How difficult is it to attain wisdom?

3. What is a man of an excellent spirit? How is this important for leadership?

PART 131 ~ VAGABONDS, PROUD ACADEMICS, AND SHAMEFUL SINNERS

Proverbs 18:1

A man who isolates himself seeks his own desire; he rages against all wise judgment. (NKJV)

Ever since Cain killed his brother, became a vagabond on the earth, and then proceeded to build the first city, natural man has sought after anonymity in the big city. When he follows the true desires of his sinful heart, he repudiates all human relationship. As the Marquis de Sade wrote, "My neighbor is nothing to me. There is not the slightest relationship between him and myself." Another modern existentialist philosopher, Jean-Paul Sartre, wrote, "Hell is other people." Thus, you can see that this self-consciously humanistic man seeks only his own desires; others just inconvenience him in this quest. This is because others might hold him accountable for his behavior. They would force him to be honest with who he is, including his selfishness and sin. Therefore, he withdraws within himself. But the more he isolates himself, the more he gives way to his own wicked desires. The consequences of such a pattern of life are frightening.

This is really the legacy of the modern cities. Men isolate themselves from the human community that might be found in smaller towns. In the end, they find themselves raging against the wise judgment they might have picked up from their fathers and grandfathers, pastors, and loved ones. Cutting themselves off from others who might check them in their sin results in the abandonment of all wisdom and an eventual breakdown of culture.

Proverbs 18:2

A fool has no delight in understanding, but that his heart may discover itself.

Have you ever met a person who seemed to be interested only in his own opinions? Whenever others shared information, he wasn't all that interested in listening. But he had the most profound respect for his own words.

How are falsehoods generated, but that fools sit around thinking up new ways of looking at reality? Somebody had to come up with the idea that a rock (or inanimate object) turned into a human being by pure chance over a billion years. This idea obviously did not originate from God's truth. This is just another vain opinion concocted in the heart of a fool who took no real delight in true understanding. Ultimately, these lies are generated in the wicked hearts of men who trust in their own hearts more than they trust in the revelation of God's Word. May God protect us from worshiping our own ideas—and from lethal pride!

Proverbs 18:3

When the wicked comes, then comes also contempt, and with ignominy reproach.

Sin always casts shame upon the one who commits it. The ungodly will do their best to deny it, hide from it, shift the blame, or atone for it according to their own terms. But they cannot rid themselves of that shame. Even within our ungodly systems, men who thought they could get away with certain sexual sins or violent crimes are marked by these crimes in newspaper reports forty years after the fact. Governments still hold the warrants for their arrest. While it is true that God forgives the worst of sinners, the criminal acts that men commit will taint their reputations for a lifetime.

If you take a cookie from the cookie jar in clear disobedience to your parent's directions, you will experience guilt for that sin. If it is discovered, you will be marked for the time being as the child who took the cookie. Of course, when the sin is made known, corrected, and forgiven, then the whole matter will eventually be forgotten. But that is because you are marked, not as a sinner, but as a *repentant* sinner. If a child fails to repent of his stealing and instead continues in a course of thievery in the home, he will eventually lose the trust of his family. Consequently, he will come to be characterized by his sin and others will consider him as one who is lacking in integrity. When whole families and communities lack character, people begin to lock their doors at night and place burglar alarm systems in their homes.

Family Discussion Questions:

1. Are we tempted to isolate ourselves from our friends and family members who might correct us in our sins? What are some of the ways in which men isolate themselves today? Do colleges usually draw us closer to the communities in which we were raised, or do they take us farther away from our communities?

2. Who are the people in our lives who would provide us with the wisest judgments?

3. Are we more confident in our own opinions concerning God's Word, or in God's Word itself? Do we listen with humility to the ideas shared by others, or are we quick to respond with our own opinions?

4. Do you listen to the opinions of others? What are the things a person might do in a conversation that would indicate that they are not really listening to others, being only interested in their own opinions?

5. Give examples of communities or nations that bear the reproach of the wicked who taught and led them.

PART 132 ~ WISE WORDS VS. FOOLISH POLICIES
Proverbs 18:4

The words of a man's mouth are as deep waters, and the wellspring of wisdom as a flowing brook.

Animals do not speak, and they do not build things or have godly families. They live in holes and leave their defecations wherever they happen to be. They do not plan for a rainy day, and are therefore subject to the conditions of their immediate environment.

But sometimes humans are not much different from animals. Left to themselves, without any true wisdom from God and His revelation, men are reduced to primitive, ungodly conditions. The difference between animals and humans consists mainly in what thoughts they think and the words they speak. Look around you, and what do you see? You see buildings, automobiles, churches, family reunions, people dressed in beautiful clothes, marriages that last for sixty years, and governments that maintain some order in a society where sinful people live together and do business with each other. None of these things would exist without wisdom, and the ability to communicate that wisdom through powerful things called "words."

Almost every person on earth will speak words and listen to words throughout his lifetime. Not all words spoken and received are fountains of pure water. Sometimes they pour out of the mouths of men like gurgling, noxious, toxic waste. After saturating their minds and ears with these ideas and words, those words will prepare people for eternal fire. Never underestimate the power of words spoken, whether they issue from a father in family devotions, a mother working in the kitchen, or a pastor who preaches from a pulpit.

Proverbs 18:5

It is not good to accept the person of the wicked, to overthrow the righteous in judgment.

At least three times thus far, this lesson has been repeated. But one of the goals of the Book of Proverbs is to give wisdom to kings, and it is the responsibility of the civil magistrate to establish order in a community.

Perhaps one of the most damaging and destructive programs ever instituted against a nation in the history of the world came under the president Lyndon B. Johnson when in the 1960s he instituted a humanist initiative called "The Great Society." Among the families living in the inner city at that time, less than 20% of the children were born without fathers. Today the rate exceeds 70%! Prior to 1960, there were few government subsidies for irresponsible and immoral people who adopted a fornicating lifestyle. Since that time, the United States government has succeeded in completely destroying the institution of the family, especially with "minority groups" who live in the inner city. By subsidizing fornication, the government encourages more fornication, and the result is the unraveling of the social fabric of the nation.

If Lyndon B. Johnson had carefully read this verse, he would have known it is not a good thing at all for a civil leader to favor the wicked in their sin. The Bible forbids favoring the poor in judgment or in taxation (Exod. 30:15), and favoring fornicators in their sin is even worse. He may have thought he was doing a good thing, but America will suffer the consequences of these unwise policies for at least another century.

Family Discussion Questions:

1. How can words be characterized as "deep waters" or "flowing brooks"? What are some of the effects of toxic words?

2. What kind of words do we listen to, and how have these words helped or hurt our family?

3. Compare two homes or two countries, and show how words really make a difference in how people live.

4. What was it about the "Great Society" that produced such devastation in the inner cities in America?

PART 133 ~ HURTFUL WORDS
Proverbs 18:6

A fool's lips enter into contention, and his mouth calls for strokes.

Were it not for foolish words, there would be no contention. There are some words that will just irritate others around us. They are words that provoke. Sometimes they are proud, bragging words in which we compare ourselves to others, goading them into a "Who-is-the-better-person?" contest.

So what do you do with somebody who runs off at the mouth? Human relationships are often tenuous things, and social units like families and churches can easily come apart when fools speak their minds. In order to maintain peace and order in the home or the community, any father or leader must stop foolish talk. Here is a definitive reason why a father and mother should use the rod or spanking paddle on their children. The tongue is an unruly member and must be properly trained; the rod is one important method by which this is done.

Proverbs 18:7

A fool's mouth is his destruction, and his lips are the snare of his soul.

Sometimes it is imprudent to discipline a fool in his foolishness. He may turn upon you with even more animus and work hard to destroy your reputation with more slander and foolish talking. Many who were subjected to attacks on the Internet have found this to be the case today. To argue with fools is akin to striking the tar baby, in which you are increasingly entangled the more you try to oppose it. It would be better to leave the fool alone. Simply ignore him in his tirade, and in time he will destroy himself.

Proverbs 18:8

The words of a talebearer are as wounds, and they go down into the innermost parts of the belly.

There is a common saying that has become, in the minds of many, a sort of truism. It says, "Sticks and stones may break my bones, but words will never hurt me." Of course, this is nothing but empty bravado and should be rejected in the face of this Proverb. Words are powerful things, either to bless or to curse, to edify or to destroy. Would you rather stick your friend in the stomach with a sword or gossip about him behind his back? Not many people have what it takes to overcome their inhibitions and stick a real knife in the body of an enemy, let alone a friend. Yet, they will use their tongues in an irresponsible way such that they will wound their friend, and perhaps even wound him for life. When you were young, your parents taught you to be careful with knives. You knew that you couldn't throw them around the kitchen willy-nilly. Certainly the tongue demands equal care. Respect the power of the tongue!

Family Discussion Questions:

1. Discuss some of the reasons why words are so powerful. In what ways can foolish words be destructive to the person speaking?

2. What is foolish talk? What sorts of things might be said in a car trip that would provoke contention and make the whole trip miserable? For what kind of talk might your parents need to discipline you?

3. How might you destroy a friendship by the use of the tongue?

PART 134 ~ DESTROYING A HERITAGE
Proverbs 18:9

He also that is slothful in his work is brother to him that is a great waster [destroyer].

During times of prosperity within some societies, there are children who inherit substantial wealth from their parents. In these societies, men and women seek to live the life of leisure. During the breakdown of the English Empire, a well-known author named P.G. Wodehouse wrote approximately ninety books, portraying, in a rather sardonic way, the lifestyles of those people who were pursuing the life of leisure and consuming the capital of previous generations. What he failed to mention is that these rich families were *destroying* the wealth of the previous generation, and they were fundamentally slothful in their character. Sadly, this is the pattern of many children who receive a spiritual or physical inheritance from their parents. By slothfulness they consume the inheritance and destroy the character of the nation.

If God blesses you with capital or inheritance, the temptation is to spend the rest of your life in a state of leisure, or in what is known as "retirement," in which you consume the capital that should be invested into the next generation. But this commitment to leisure becomes corrosive to the character of both the elderly and the subsequent generations who will emulate them. So while the elderly are busy playing their golf games twenty hours a week, the young men are playing their computer games for forty hours! Is it any surprise that, according to a *Newsweek* magazine article published in 2008, 70% of young men are not grown up by thirty years of age, up from 30% in 1970?[2] As America faces a fractured economy under an unprecedented debt load of $100 trillion dollars in the first part of the 21st century, we must attribute such destruction to a national spirit of slothfulness, encouraged along by a general worldview of leisure, retirement, and "social security" provided by government.

2 http://www.newsweek.com/2008/08/30/why-i-am-leaving-guyland.html

If you have been blessed with capital, an inheritance, or a savings account, this only means that you are more responsible before God to invest that capital and do something productive with it for the sake of the kingdom of God!

Family Discussion Questions:

1. If the life of leisure is not a biblical approach to life, what is the kind of life God wants us to live?

2. How much are we striving for a life of leisure? What is our attitude toward work?

3. If you were to inherit substantial wealth from your parents, what would you do with it?

PART 135 ~ A GOOD DEFENSE
Proverbs 18:10

The name of the LORD is a strong tower: the righteous runs into it, and is safe.

Every worldview has its theory of sin and salvation. In other words, practically everybody will admit that man has problems and needs to be saved. The disagreement is on how to define man's basic problem, and then how he is saved from that problem! The Book of Proverbs is a little Bible, in that it contains the basic truths of a biblical worldview in capsule form. Man's basic problem is sin, and all of the violence and corruption in the world can be linked to his sinful condition. Of course, sin is rebelling against God and transgressing His law. But how are we saved from this predicament? The answer is given in this little verse. By running to God, we are saved from the evil that would destroy us!

Salvation is found in the name of the Lord. This means that we trust in the reputation of God, believing in what the Bible says about Him. We hang all of our hopes on what the words on a piece of paper say about the goodness of God, the history of God's work in redemption, and the promises of God. It is our trust in God's reputation. It is our faith that saves.

Proverbs 18:11

The rich man's wealth is his strong city, and as an high wall in his own conceit.

Jesus said that we would always have the poor in our midst. Despite the utopian ideas of the Marxists who insist upon an egalitarian society, the undeniable reality of life is that there will always be those who are blessed with more wealth than others. There is a certain value in wealth, and this passage mentions one of them. Riches provide protection. As a walled city protects its citizens from marauding bands, so wealth protects a man and his family from the enemies of hunger, poverty, disease, and legal assaults. Generally speaking, rich people can protect themselves from lawsuits by hiring expensive lawyers. They might even be able to protect themselves from debilitating diseases by means of expensive insurance programs. In most Western countries today, the vast majority of the people are rich and hardly know what it would be like to be poor. They have built multiple layers of secure walls to protect themselves from every sort of catastrophe. Their security is found in their own savings accounts and government-mandated social security. They are supremely confident men—confident in themselves and in their own wealth. This is why wealthy people see no need for God. They are confident in their own abilities, their own economic systems, and their own corporations, banks, and governments.

Proverbs 18:12

Before destruction the heart of man is haughty, and before honor is humility.

What happens to those wealthy men who build their empires and expand their wealth? For a century or two these men may ignore God in their conceit. After all, they have no need for

Him! Their universities, entertainment industries, businesses, and governments promote godless humanism, all the time building substantial wealth and security for them! At the moment man's pride is at its zenith, when the largest towers have been built, and all recognition of God has been utterly purged from the university textbooks, God brings these towers down. He utterly destroys their proud institutions and economies. Those high walls and strong cities that seemed so impregnable always come crashing down! In the last several centuries, what once were proud humanist empires have now ceased to exist, including the magnificent powers of Spain (16th century), France (18th century), and England (19th century). When will men learn to fear God and trust only Him for their physical and spiritual salvation?

All of us will die someday. How will our own abilities and our own wealth save us in that terrible day? It behooves us to not give way to pride for even a single day in our lives, but rather we must place our trust in God alone (verse 10).

Family Discussion Questions:

1. In what ways can slothfulness be destructive to a person?

2. Where do we put our trust? Do we trust in God or in our own wealth and strength?

3. Should we build our castle walls with insurance programs, retirement programs, and social security programs in order to shelter ourselves from catastrophes? Why do we build these walls of defense?

4. How might we be sure that wealth and material blessing never displace our worship and trust in the living God?

PART 136 ~ WISE COUNSELORS AND WOUNDED SPIRITS

Proverbs 18:13

He that answers a matter before he hears it, it is folly and shame unto him.

The scenario is all too common. In the middle of a marital crisis, a wife complains to a counselor or friend about how badly her husband treats her. Of course, the temptation for the counselor is to quickly take sides in the conflict before hearing both sides of the story.

The temptation to rely on only one side in the conflict is sometimes overwhelming. This is especially true when you have a closer relationship with the first party arguing his or her case. But to give in to this temptation is foolish and undermines your own integrity and reputation. Wise counselors quickly learn that there are always two sides to a story. Moreover, these conflicts can be very complex due to the layers of deceit and wickedness that lie within human hearts.

What is commended here in this passage is patience, careful investigation, and contemplation before giving advice. It is usually your pride that wants to "jump the gun" in order that others might hear your opinions and "sage wisdom." But you should rather develop the habit of asking questions. Dig deeper. If you sense that someone may be lying or exaggerating, take a little more time to investigate the matter before you provide your counsel.

Proverbs 18:14

The spirit of a man will sustain his infirmity; but who can bear a wounded spirit?

While climbing one of the largest mountains in the Western hemisphere several years ago, a mountaineer fell into a deep ravine. His partner left him, thinking he was dead. The climber had broken both of his legs, but he pulled himself over ice and rock with his hands for six full days, eventually making it to his base camp! Stories like this illustrate the incredible strength available within the inner spirit of a human being. Men have overcome debilitating handicaps by sheer strength of spirit, accomplishing the most amazing feats.

But then there is the man of the strongest physical constitution whose spirit is wounded to the very core of his being. He may lose his beloved wife and never fully recover from the blow. He would rather have been tossed 1,000 feet by a large truck than for his spirit to take a stunning blow of that magnitude. It would be better to lose the use of your hands, arms, legs, and feet, rather than to sustain a wound to the spirit. Who can bear a wounded spirit? There is only one thing to do with a wounded spirit—take it to the Lord Himself. In the words of the Psalmist, "Hope in God. For I shall yet praise Him who is the help of my countenance and my God!"

As long as his spirit is intact, a man may be able to fend for himself. But when the spirit has been shot through by the convicting Word of God, or by hard providential dealings (the loss of a wife or a child), a man will come to the end of himself! There is now nothing within his power that can save him. If he would realize this and turn to God for help, then he might be saved out of his desperate condition.

Family Discussion Questions:

1. What does it mean to have a wounded spirit?

2. What happens when a man does not patiently investigate both sides of the story before he makes a judgment call?

3. Why is it so tempting to give counsel before we have heard all sides of the story and carefully contemplated the problems?

4. What are some of the signals that people might be exaggerating as they tell their "side of the story"?

5. How might you counsel one who has been wounded in spirit?

PART 137 ~ WISE AND INFLUENTIAL MEN
Proverbs 18:15

The heart of the prudent gets knowledge; and the ear of the wise seeks knowledge.

Do you ever get tired of listening to the same sermons and reading the same Word every day? After ten, twenty, or thirty years of listening to the same Word, you would think that you have heard it all! This kind of spirit runs in conflict with the lesson contained in this verse. At the point where you feel like you have heard it all and you know it all, that is where you have abandoned true prudence and wisdom. If you will be truly wise, you must have the motivation to seek it, to dig for it. Those who want diamonds and gold will not find them lying on the surface of the ground. They have to dig for them, and sometimes they dig hundreds and thousands of feet into the earth. The search for wisdom requires the same diligence. When listening to a sermon, you need to pull out a pick and a shovel and go to work. Do not rely upon the teacher to do all the work. If there is no motivation on your part to seek out the wisdom God has for you—if you will not aggressively listen to the Word—you will never mine the big six-ounce nuggets of gold. The first few years you listened to the Word and learned, you may have obtained the easy lessons. But the longer you pursue the faith, the more work you'll have to put into it to find the mother lode.

Proverbs 18:16

A man's gift makes room for him, and brings him before great men.

There are many reasons to give gifts. Even selfish materialists give gifts because they know that gifts will open doors for them. Whether it be a business lunch or a campaign donation, relationships are generally improved by gifts. This is not to say that all gifts are ethically appropriate, for elsewhere the Book of Proverbs condemns the bribery that perverts justice. Sometimes campaign donations are meant to solicit government subsidies and an inequitable, preferential treatment. Certainly this ought to be avoided, but this should not discourage all gift-giving. Is it inappropriate to give your legislative representative a gift certificate to a restaurant for him and his wife? There are laws today that control these things, but if your intention is to warm up the legislator to listen to you as you encourage him to support godly policies, then there is nothing inherently immoral about such gift giving.

Proverbs 18:17

He that is first in his own cause seems just; but his neighbor comes and searches him.

In any conflict between neighbors or brothers, a wise judge or a wise mother will always listen to both sides of the story before making a judgment. That is because men will always tend to present themselves in the best light. Whether it is two brothers arguing over a toy, or two businessmen arguing over a contract, it is rare to find somebody who will quickly admit to his own sins in a conflict and take responsibility for them. Otherwise, he probably would not have sinned against his neighbor in the first place!

We do not admit to the true wickedness of heart and action because we are blind to these things! By nature, we instinctively cover up our sins by rationalizations, or we just refuse to honestly assess our own heart motivations. In other words, our weak spots are almost always in our blind spot! We can't be honest with others about ourselves because we can't be honest with ourselves. This is why it is so important for somebody else to take a look at us from the outside. As a wise counselor or judge listens to both sides of the story and examines the evidence, often he can uncover the true facts of the case and identify the true heart motives at work.

Family Discussion Questions:

1. Can we ever exhaust the wisdom of God's Word? What then should be our attitude as we read and hear the Word of God?

2. How aggressive is our family in the pursuit of wisdom? Do we mine for gold in the sermons we hear each Sunday at church? What are some of the ways in which we can better pursue wisdom as we study God's Word?

3. What is legitimate gift giving in business and politics?

4. Why do we have a hard time admitting our own sins in conflicts?

PART 138 ~ RESOLVING CONFLICTS
Proverbs 18:18

The lot causes contentions to cease, and parts between the mighty.

Some disagreements may be worked out easily. But others can be extremely difficult for many reasons. There may be long-standing animosities, or there may be layers and layers of deceit working throughout the discussions. Or it may be impossible to really ascertain the facts of the case. The fellow that saw what happened may have died, for example. There may also be equal fault on both sides, making it impossible to favor one side over the other.

It is important for the wisest judges to assume humility at some point, admitting they cannot administer perfect justice. Only God is both omniscient and absolutely just, so only He can make the wisest judgments. In light of that, human judges may sometimes flip a coin to determine who should win a case. Yet if parents, elders, or civil judges did that sort of thing, it is a dereliction of duty—an abdication of human responsibility. You may remember that Proverbs 16:33 established the absolute sovereignty of God in every roll of the dice or flip of the coin. Moreover, the hearts of kings and judges are in the hands of God, and He turns them wherever He wishes (Prov. 21:1). Therefore, it is true that God is 100% sovereign over the outcome of the decision whether a flip of a coin is used or not. But when men resort to the flip of a coin in every single case, before they have attempted to consider the case and make a righteous judgment in the matter, they have abdicated their responsibility. Nevertheless, if they have exhausted all of their own abilities and applied as much human responsibility to the case as possible to obtain justice, a judge may flip a coin and turn the case entirely over to the sovereign direction of God.

If both parties are willing to submit themselves to the flip of a coin, it becomes difficult then for either party to take issue with the judge or with the other party after the coin drops to the floor. The decision was made by the providential outcome of the lot. No matter how sure they are of themselves in their opinions concerning the case, and no matter how powerful these men are, they must bow to the sovereignty of God in the outcome of the coin toss.

Proverbs 18:19

A brother offended is harder to be won than a strong city: and their contentions are like the bars of a castle.

Have you ever tried to salvage a vase that was smashed into a thousand pieces? Or have you tried to rescue a ship that was sinking and already ten feet under the water? Some catastrophic events take us past "the point of no return." If the vase had only chipped a little we might have repaired it. Or, if the ship had only a foot or two of water in the hold, we might have been able to man the pumps for a while and salvage the craft. The same principle applies to human relationships. It is possible to sink a relationship such that salvage would be nearly impossible.

Think about how hard it would have been to take down a walled city before the days of aircraft and cannons. Such a tremendous feat required wise planning, indomitable courage, and persistent endeavor. No less effort is required to win a brother who is offended! In these conflicts, hearts really grow harder than concrete and tougher than steel.

Above all, you must work hard to maintain and mend your relationships before things come unraveled. Don't drop the vase, and don't sink the ship. If you have offended a brother, humble yourself and go to your brother immediately, confessing your sins and asking for his forgiveness. Do not delay for a moment when it comes to manning the pumps in the hold of the ship! There are some things you can afford to put off until later, but Jesus requires you to mend your relationships the minute you sense your brother is offended with you (Matt. 5:23–24).

Is there any hope for broken relationships? If there is hope for the broken relationship between man and his eternal Creator, and if there is any power in the reconciling work of the Son of God, then we have to believe that His blood can dissolve those iron bars separating brother from brother! However, if there are unbelievers involved in the conflict, there is very little hope that it can ever be resolved. Professing Christians who live in bitterness toward one another and refuse to restore relationships have not experienced the reconciling power of the blood of Christ. Reconciliation in our vertical relationship with God is concomitant with reconciliation in the horizontal with our brothers and sisters in the body of Christ.

Family Discussion Questions:

1. What types of situations are legitimate for the use of lots or the flip of a coin?

2. Have you ever flipped a coin to make a decision? Was this an appropriate thing to do? What are the right situations in which you might do this?

3. How effective are we at maintaining our relationships in our family and church? Are there any relationships that need repair right now?

4. Are there any relationships in our lives that are in need of serious work? What would you do if you had a long-standing, difficult conflict like that described in verse 19?

PART 139 ~ THE POWER OF WORDS
Proverbs 18:20

A man's belly shall be satisfied with the fruit of his mouth; and with the increase of his lips shall he be filled.

The power of the mouth to produce much good in life is beyond your wildest imagination! Of course, the converse is just as true. The tongue is a world of iniquity and is set on fire of hell (James 3:6). In the beautiful mountains of southwest Oregon, you can find thousands of acres of ugly, barren mountain range. Several decades ago, someone was driving his truck up in the mountains, and his catalytic converter touched off a spark that set that world on fire and burned down miles of beautiful forest. Such is the destructive capability of the tongue.

Yet, the power of the tongue to produce the fruit of a thousand orchards is the emphasis in this passage. It all depends on whether we can learn to use it properly. As the words we speak nurture our relationships, strengthen the character of those we edify, and properly apply God's principles to our dominion tasks, we will see God's material blessings upon our families, our church, and our wider community.

For related commentary, reference Proverbs 12:14.

Proverbs 18:21

Death and life are in the power of the tongue: and they that love it shall eat the fruit thereof.

It is practically impossible to overstate the power of the spoken word! While we know that God is sovereign over life and death, heaven and hell, our words still make a difference. Should you see a prostitute regenerated or a cannibal come to Christ in some distant island, you know it is the fruit of a missionary who took the time to teach these people the Gospel of Christ. What makes our children any different from a drug-addicted, thieving juvenile in New York City? Of course, it is the grace of God. But it is also the careful, loving teaching that comes from caring parents.

Consider two identical plants in a garden. One is dried, and the other is flourishing and blossoming. There are a number of factors that play into the health of a plant. But if one of the plants has been watered for six weeks, and the other was deprived of all water, I'm sure one could conclude that water makes a difference. The effect of water is powerful in the life of a plant! So it is with the discipleship of our children. Watering them with the Word of God does make a real difference. Some children will go to hell and some will go to heaven—and the words spoken to them do contribute to their final destination. Choose your words carefully.

If you visit a youth group or school attended by children of varied backgrounds, you will quickly notice the difference between those children who have been discipled by the fruitful words of God and those who have essentially been left to themselves to be discipled by popular culture. There is a stark difference in heart attitudes, spiritual disciplines, and the fruits of the Spirit versus the fruits of the flesh.

Sadly, not everyone who hears the good words of a faithful preacher will profit from them. Not every plant receives the water because it sits in hard and rocky soil that will not absorb water. First, the soil of the heart must be prepared to hear the convicting message of the Gospel, if the plant is to bear fruit. The Apostle Paul calls the feet of the faithful messengers of the Gospel "beautiful" (Rom. 10:15), but what about the ears of those who are willing to hear? They are blessed ears indeed, blessed by God Himself! *They that love it, shall eat the fruit thereof.*

Proverbs 18:22

*Whoso finds a wife finds a good thing, and obtains favour of the
LORD.*

There is nothing more important in a young man's life than
finding a suitable wife to help him in his dominion task and to
be his loving and faithful companion until death. When God
created the man, he was only half a man until God brought
him a wife. The wife completes the husband. With only a few
exceptions, a man without a wife is insufficient for the task of
managing his household economy, raising children, engaging
in hospitality, or shepherding families in a church. Now, in
the modern corporate economy where each individual is
subservient to a large, bureaucratic, government-regulated
corporation, families have been fragmented. Husbands do
not need to depend on their wives in an economic sense, and
neither do wives depend on their husbands for security. All are
dependent upon the state and state-regulated institutions.

The task of finding a wife is no insignificant thing. From a
child's early years, we ought to bathe that matter in prayer, for
ultimately it is God Who will guide a young man to the right
spouse. Once he finds that wife, for the rest of his life he must
consider this woman a precious gift from God. Should a man
ever despise the gift God has given him, then, of course, he is
despising the Giver Himself.

Family Discussion Questions:

1. There are a number of things in life that are very powerful, yet
   very difficult to train. As the Proverbs remind us repeatedly, the
   tongue is a good example of this phenomenon. Give several other
   illustrations of this.

2. What are some things a man should look for in a wife? Why is
   finding a wife something that obtains favor from the Lord?

3. How might we help our sons find good wives? How might we
   best prepare our daughters to be godly, helpful wives to their own
   husbands?

PART 140 ~ TREASURING RELATIONSHIPS
Proverbs 18:23

The poor uses entreaties; but the rich answers roughly.

The biblical worldview maintains a sharp contrast to the Marxist worldview which dominates most developed nations today. The Marxist finds it morally unacceptable whenever some people possess more wealth than others, so the forces equalization through redistribution. From a biblical perspective, however, there is nothing wrong with material inequities. Some will be poor, and some will be rich, and it is not for men to call this a "problem" or to work to rid the world of it.

In a socialist society driven by envy, you will find slothfulness, disrespect, and a collapse of character and manners. This is because the poor no longer feel any need for the rich, either for their charitable contributions or for business opportunities. After all, if the government is redistributing the wealth and handing out jobs, who needs to maintain good working relationships with wealthy business owners?

When a man is poor, he cannot afford to lose any of the business relationships he has cultivated. To lose these relationships might mean bankruptcy or even starvation for his family. Meanwhile, a rich man who has plenty of business and $500,000 in the bank feels as if he can rest on his laurels. Often rich people do not take the time to cultivate relationships. They are too busy making money. This is more the case today in wealthy Western nations than anywhere else. The average person's relationships with family and church community are fairly weak, largely because he feels he has sufficient wealth (either through his own savings accounts or through government social security programs) to sustain him through hard times.

The desire for financial gain can sometimes cause the watering down of a congregation's character. For example, a pastor may wish to correct his congregation in their sins, risking their disapprobation. But a pastor who is in debt for his house and relies heavily on a salary from the church may be less likely to speak firmly and directly to the church. The pursuit of money is the cause of much of modern Christianity's problems.

Proverbs 18:24

A man that has friends must show himself friendly: and there is a friend that sticks closer than a brother.

Seeking friendships does not produce friends, for those who seek friendships often find themselves friendless. But those who are friendly will soon find good friends all around them! Friendships cannot be formed on a *quid pro quo* basis. For example, someone should not give gifts and exercise hospitality with the expectation that those things will be returned in kind. He may find this helpful in the cultivation of business relationships, but it doesn't work for true friendships.

The Bible does not prescribe a certain minimum number of friends. Because of differences in personalities, some people will have more friends than others. No matter what, there is value placed on the "friend that sticks closer than a brother." Good friendships tend to be somewhat tenuous in the present age, due to the transient nature of modern life. The friends we knew in our early years are not the same friendships we developed in college. After moving through five different churches in three different communities over twenty years, it would be hard to develop any life-long friends who would stick closer than a brother! If we cultivated close friendships in the places where we live, perhaps we would be a little more hesitant to move all the time! Friendships should be worth something to us. Certainly they should mean far more to us than material wealth.

Family Discussion Questions:

1. What sort of manners should we use to construct good business relationships in our work? Is it ever appropriate to speak "roughly" or "rudely" to others?

2. In what situations might we be hesitant to speak in a confrontational manner?

3. What are you doing to cultivate friendships? How do you show yourself friendly?

PART 141 ~ FOOLISH HEARTS AND LIPS
Proverbs 19:1

Better is the poor that walks in his integrity, than he that is perverse in his lips, and is a fool.

There is some blessing to material prosperity, but there are also some things that are more important than riches. Compare the whole lot of rich politicians and international bankers, manipulating the money supply to their own benefit, with some poor honest man who sells his apples from a fruit stand, carefully calibrating his scale every morning to be sure he doesn't shortchange his customers. That poor man may live in a 300 square-foot cottage, but you would much rather live that man's life than live a dishonest charade with politicians and bankers. Dishonesty may pay for a while. The car salesman who lies to his customers may succeed for a few years, but eventually the entire community will have figured out the character of this man. In some large cities and countries, these men may stay in business a very long time; but there is only so much that mass advertising can do. Without repeat customers, there is no way he will successfully compete with those of better reputations. Of course, when corrupt governments uphold corrupt industries and banking systems, honest men will have to content themselves with fewer rewards. But when the inevitable economic collapse comes upon the corrupt systems, it will be the poor, honest men who will survive.

Proverbs 19:2

Also, that the soul be without knowledge, it is not good; and he that hastes with his feet sins.

When the Bible speaks of the soul, it includes the inner being of the person: the inner motivations, the emotions, and the will. But if a soul desires and acts without knowledge, it will take the wrong direction in life. This is how the Christian faith has broken down in the West over the last several centuries. Well-intentioned, enthusiastic Christians with precious little understanding of the Word have taken the Gospel around the globe. They relied on pure emotion and enthusiasm, creating a faith that was, as some put it, "a mile wide and an inch deep." This became the seedbed for cults and rapid apostasy in the next generations. Throughout the Gospels, Jesus chastised the Jewish leaders numerous times for their lack of familiarity with the Old Testament Scriptures (Matt. 21:42; Luke 6:3; etc.). Of course, our Lord also requires a thorough knowledge of the Old and New Testaments from His teachers in the present day. Immaturity among our leaders is dangerous and sets the stage for the breakdown of faith and culture.

There is no excuse for ignorance. Should you quickly set out to do something without first thinking through your motivations and God's will as communicated through His Word, you will find yourself in all sorts of trouble. Because by nature we are sinners, it is only by a renewal of our minds in the Word of God that we will be able to live in the perfect will of God (Rom. 12:2). Therefore, it is incumbent on all of us to carefully reflect on God's Word before acting, instead of giving way to emotional impulses and fleshly inclinations.

Proverbs 19:3

The foolishness of man perverts his way: and his heart frets against the LORD.

Life is a journey. All who have ever lived traverses the journey, and the roads they take in life will either take them into the pit of destruction or to the gates of heaven. Some of the most promising, intelligent, and successful men on earth will walk a path that takes them over the cliff of destruction.

Nowadays we have these wonderful instruments called "GPS navigation systems" for cars. A computer generated voice instructs the driver along the way to his destination. As it turns out, the computers are not always accurate in their instructions, as witnessed by one driver who was told to take a right-hand turn, driving straight into a lake!

Now what will navigate the journey of a man's life? What is it that directs him along the way to the pit of destruction? Of course, it is the foolishness of his own heart. It is a heart that is hopelessly biased against its Creator! Since he refuses to worship and fear the true and living God, he must commit his life to arguing against God's existence or relevance, or His right to be God. It is this fundamental bent of his heart against God that guides his path in life. For a time it may appear that he has set a good direction, but ultimately his heart will lead him far astray.

Family Discussion Questions:

1. Can you imagine a point at which we may have to simplify our lives by surrendering a contract or quitting a job in order to salvage our integrity? Describe a possible scenario where this might happen in our family.

2. How important is emotion and enthusiasm in our worship, compared to the careful study of the Word of God and application of it to our lives? Do we have sufficient emotion and enthusiasm? Do we apply ourselves carefully to learning the Word of God and the doctrines therein?

3. What does your relationship with God look like? Are you trying to hide from God? Do you have a chip on your shoulder against God? Or do you love God and appreciate the teaching of His Word?

PART 142 ~ THE PROBLEMS OF POVERTY AND FALSE WITNESSES
Proverbs 19:4

Wealth makes many friends; but the poor is separated from his neighbor.

Sadly enough, impoverished neighborhoods are often the seedbeds of illegitimacy, drug use, and crime. Usually, the rich want to separate themselves from these social settings. Yet it seems that the miserable curses that facilitate the breakdown of character in poor societies quickly seep into the rich neighborhoods as well.

The beggars you find on street corners in large cities are typically very alone. They may have cast off their families through drunkenness or fits of violent anger. In most cases, they refuse to maintain close relationships in a church, where brothers and sisters would address their character issues and attempt to hold them accountable. Meanwhile, our state-based social systems discourage a charity that is local, relational, and voluntary; this further isolates the poor from those who could help them.

So how does one "fix" this problem of the poor? While Jesus Christ made a ministry out of helping the helpless, He assured His disciples at the end that "the poor you will always have with you." Truly, He did not come to fix the problem of poverty. He came to fix the problem of *sin*! Nevertheless, the church community is to be made up of rich and poor alike. The rich are to give of their goods generously to those in need, while retaining mutually accountable, respectful, and loving relationships within the body of the church. Because those who are wealthy have more resources and time to serve others, they will have more "friends." But a warm and relational church should provide the best opportunity for the integration of society, which is much better than the forced redistribution of wealth, forced integration of school systems, and similar programs. Although the principle in this proverb can still apply within the New Testament era church, you will be less likely to find it in the world today.

Proverbs 19:5

A false witness shall not be unpunished, and he that speaks lies shall not escape.

Occasionally, the media will report on a murder case in which an innocent man was executed for the crime he did not commit. After the fact, some witness admits to having provided false testimony in the court trial. Humanists seek solutions to problems by insisting on perfect justice, which usually involves both the incorporation of the police state on one hand (with cameras tracking every move you make), and a softening of the penalties and the total minimization of the ethical import of human crimes on the other hand. In other words, man will turn to both tyranny and anarchy in order to establish his "utopia" of perfect justice. This is all based on the assumption that there is no God Who is the very standard of justice and righteousness. Man creates his own sham justice when he denies God's standard.

But what do *we* say about the innocent man executed because of false testimony given in court? Of course, biblical law requires that a man offering such testimony in a murder trial be subject to the death penalty himself (Deut. 19:16–18). If our courts would maintain biblical laws on witnesses in court, we would have far fewer of these cases. Moreover, biblical law requires that *every matter* be established on the account of *two or three* witnesses. But in the ultimate sense, we trust that there is a God Whose eyes are everywhere, "beholding the evil and the good," and perfect justice will be established in the courts of heaven. We are not cosmic dust floating about in a causeless, material universe. We are moral creatures, created with a strong sense of justice—*because we are created in the image of God,* Who Himself is the very standard of justice. We must believe that this God is capable of administering perfect justice in the realm of time and eternity. No false witness will ever escape His purview, no matter how carefully he covers his footsteps.

Family Discussion Questions:

1. How do we "fix" the problem of poverty?

2. How well do we integrate poorer people in our church assembly?

3. What is the biblical punishment for a false witness in a trial?

4. What happens to the man who bears false witness in a trial, but nobody catches him at it?

5. Knowing that God will administer justice in the end, how does this affect the way that you react to injustices?

PART 143 ~ THE PRINCE AND THE POOR
Proverbs 19:6

Many will entreat the favor of the prince, and every man is a friend to him that gives gifts.

Everybody wants to get ahead in life. So when a certain person is in control of who gets promoted, that person will be the recipient of many entreaties. People know where the "bread is buttered," and you can be sure they will butter up the fellow who holds all the butter! Of course, those who sit in the place of influence face the temptation to give way to bribery and to deal unjustly. The temptation to pride is even greater. When a man is in a place of power, he often forgets his own obligations to his superiors and to God Himself. A man never has the right to pervert justice to his own ends, even if he stands to benefit from those who give him gifts and honor.

Proverbs 19:7

All the brethren of the poor do hate him: how much more do his friends
go far from him? He pursues them with words, yet they [abandon]
him.

This verse presents an even more severe indictment on the
poor man than did verse 4 of this chapter. Not only does he
fail to win many friends, but here we read that his brothers
withdraw from him. He can't even curry the favor of his own
brothers! To accurately grasp the scenario, you must define the
poor as the truly indigent poor—those without the means to
provide for their basic needs, such as shelter and food. These
are the blind beggars on the side of the road, the maimed at
the pool of Bethesda.

When a man has sunk to the bottom of society due to his
misfortunes, his addictions, his gambling, his homosexuality,
or other destructive habits, it is not uncommon for his own
brothers to "give up on him." Occasionally, they may toss a
few dollars his way, but they soon discover that they cannot fix
his fundamental problem, whatever it happens to be. So they
abandon him. They don't invite him over for the holidays,
especially if he is likely to be an unhealthy influence on their
families.

As Christians, we do not want to countenance sins in others,
but we also must be careful to minister to those in need. In
the New Testament we find Christ treating the immediate
physical need of the sick, but then He instructs them to "sin
no more" (John 5:1–15). He is careful not to separate the
spiritual needs of a man from his physical needs, for His real
agenda is to see complete healing in both body and soul of the
poor and needy. Though we ourselves are not the Lord Christ
Who is sovereign in healing, we do what we can for our poor
relatives. We should, for example, provide needed shelter and
food for our needy mothers or grandmothers (1 Tim. 5:8ff).
Nevertheless, we should not support able-bodied men who
just refuse to work, for as the Apostle says, "If a man will not
work, neither shall he eat" (2 Thess. 2:10).

Christ crossed a universe to reach out to the poor and needy. If this be the case, we should be able to cross a city to find the ones who need to hear the message of the Gospel. There is no question that the circumstances of poor people and the sin that often proliferates in poor districts create distance. But we ought to always be ready to cross that divide to carry the good news of the Gospel. Should the message be rejected, the distance between us remains. Still, we should always be those attempting to reach out across the chasms in order to seek a unity that is only possible in subjection to Christ (Gal. 3:28). We love the strangers in order that they might love Christ (Heb. 13:2)!

Family Discussion Questions:

1. Should we be extra friendly to the person in charge of hiring or handing out business contracts and promotions in the work place?

2. How is a person reduced to severe poverty? Is it due to his lack of character or other reasons?

3. What sorts of poor people can we effectively help? Are there any poor people that we cannot or should not help?

PART 144 ⁓ FOOLS AND FALSE WITNESSES
Proverbs 19:8

He that gets wisdom loves his own soul: he that keeps understanding shall find good.

It is amazing how quickly young men are drawn into the company of fools! They sit at the feet of "wise" fools in the university, impressed by their neat rhetorical devices and their abilities to turn phrases this way or that. They are easily drawn into a culture that takes God's creative forms, twisting them toward violating His law-order. Instead of reproving the unfruitful works of rebellion, existentialism, nihilism, and other ungodly systems of thought, they slowly amalgamate into them.

The problem with these young men is that they hate their own souls! Have you ever seen anyone who hated his right hand so much that he cut it off? It is one thing to hate your right hand or your left foot, but what crazy person would hate his own soul? This is a form of insanity. Instead of seeking out ungodly influences in your life, you must seek out godly teachers who will lead you in the paths of wisdom. For the love of your soul, you must do this!

Proverbs 19:9

A false witness shall not be unpunished, and he that speaks lies shall perish.

Here is a severe warning for the man who perpetuates lying. "He that speaks lies shall perish." Although the Old Testament has little or nothing to say about the eternal state after death, the book of Revelation provides a clearer picture. There is a life after death, but not every person will make it into heaven. According to Revelation 22:15, outside the heavenly city are "sorcerers, whoremongers, murderers, and idolators, and whosoever loves and makes a lie." And leaving no room for equivocation on the matter, the book of the apocalypse further declares that "all liars shall have their part in the lake which burns with fire and brimstone: which is the second death" (Rev. 21:8). These grim passages should, at the least, cause us to take the matter of lying seriously. But would God condemn a child to hell for lying to his mother about whether he removed a cookie from the cookie jar? This is, of course, a serious matter, for if a small boy begins his career of lying in this way and continues in this vein for a lifetime, he will most certainly be consigned to the flames of hell. While it is not a single lie that defines a liar, the heart that loves the lie is the determinant factor. Naturally, it is a string of lies that proceed from the heart of a liar. Unless the liar repents of his love for lies, and, by God's grace, can see that he is lying to himself by being in rebellion against God, he will most certainly burn in hell forever. A Christian may lie occasionally, but if his heart has been sanctified by the Spirit, he will hate those lies and repent of them.

For related commentary, reference Proverbs 19:5.

Proverbs 19:10

Delight is not seemly for a fool; much less for a servant to have rule over princes.

There are some things that are wise and fitting and others that are not. To seek to perpetuate that which is unwise and unfitting is to do wrong. This is one reason why the Bible discourages the plowing of an ox and a donkey together. We do not have the right to act like idiots.

Now suppose that a building contractor characteristically rewards his laziest and most unproductive employee with a trip to Hawaii each year, but he provides no such benefit to any of his other more productive employees. To make this a regular practice is not only foolish but also sinful and destructive to the work of true dominion.

Sadly, many large social systems have adopted Marxist thought, seeking after something called "social justice." It is based on the idea that everybody should enjoy equal pay and equal status. However, the foolishness of egalitarian Marxism is obvious when you consider that not everybody is of equal character to merit equal pay and status in life. While it is true that income level is no true indication of the character of a person, it is terribly unwise to attempt to take wealth from a person. Nor is it wise to elect men of little character and self-control to high public office. Even within democratic societies, these men quickly destroy their reputations and bring shame upon themselves and their electorates. Americans will doubtless always remember the character weaknesses of President Bill Clinton and his penchant for womanizing while he filled the highest office in the country. If men of low character are appointed to authoritative position in business, they often abuse their employees, make unwise decisions, and generally fail to lead with vision and wisdom. Such foolish men will drive their businesses and nations into the ground.

Family Discussion Questions:

1. If you loved your body, would you want to feed it from time to time? What about your soul? How would you feed your soul?

2. Have you been telling more lies lately? Are you turning into a habitual liar? Do you find your lies giving birth to more lies? Why is it such a frightening thing for us to give way to a habit of lying?

3. Is everybody of equal character in life? What happens when you reward somebody with riches, power, and comfort, but he does not have the character to handle it?

PART 145 ~ GETTING ANGRY
Proverbs 19:11

The discretion of a man defers his anger; and it is his glory to pass over a transgression.

Somebody once said that the last man to get angry in an argument wins. The assumption here is that any form of anger or indignation is always inappropriate, and the person who is the least affected by emotion is the cool, persuasive, even-tempered logician and the most persuasive. This is a bit over-simplified for the lesson at hand. Passion does have a place in human existence—even a passion rooted in conviction and a love of the truth. But when men are governed by hot emotions, they are not governed by a love for God. Certainly we should not equate love for God to the emotion of anger. These are not the same thing. Occasionally, a love for God might produce indignation toward some injustice, such as when Jesus overturned the moneychangers' tables in the temple. But any form of indignation apart from a love for

God is self-centered irritation and can only be described as sinful anger. Moreover, emotion untempered and undirected by careful and thoughtful consideration of the circumstances in the situation, and the principles of God's Word that apply, will inevitably result in unwise words and actions. The man of discretion will defer anger as much as possible. As James puts it, the wise man is quick to hear, slow to speak, and slow to anger (James 1:19). When he sets out to overturn the tables in the temple, he does so after careful preconsideration of his actions, with a full understanding of the perceptions and risks related to what he is doing. So we find Jesus taking the time to make a whip of cords, deliberately planning out his actions.

People are always sinning against each other. This is the nature of human relationships. That is why forgiveness is part of the warp and woof of life. When Jesus told His disciples that they must forgive 490 times, He was by no means exaggerating. It is possible that you may have to forgive somebody as many as 490 times in a single month! Most sins are minor and should drop off of us like water off a duck's back. Occasionally, we may have to lovingly confront a brother in the manner prescribed in Matthew 18:15–17. But you have to be careful with this. If you confronted every single person in your life every time he sinned, you would be confronting people all day long. Moreover, others would have to confront you constantly as well. How would you like that to happen? We must be patient with others, and treat others as we would like to be treated ourselves. And nobody wants to be confronted with his own sin on a continual, perpetual basis. Much of our lives must be taken up with overlooking minor sins and faults. Blessed are the merciful, for they shall obtain mercy. It takes an honorable, magnanimous man to overlook the sins of others and learn to work with fallible, sinful human beings.

Proverbs 19:12

The king's wrath is as the roaring of a lion; but his favor is as dew upon the grass.

Imagine that you are camping out in the brush of wild Africa, and you hear a lion's roar just a few yards from where you sit. Can you think of anything more frightening? Grown lions are intimidating animals, but an angry lion in close proximity to you and your comrades is an almost unthinkable horror because the potential for destruction to life is real and imminent. So it is with angry kings.

Some may remember those sardonic lyrics from a popular song of the rebellious 1960s—"I fought the law, but the law won." Generally, it does no good to provoke a king to wrath (Prov. 20:2). When a Christian must conscientiously disagree with the policy of a company or a country, he does so at his own risk. Civil disobedience is only a temporary measure. Should a magistrate forbid you to preach the Gospel in a certain town, you may have to flee the wrath of the civil magistrate to other cities or countries.

On the other hand, if the heart of the king or the civil magistrate turns in favor toward your mission work, you may be able to establish churches or Bible studies in those companies or countries without fear of reprisal. Thanks to the First Amendment in the United States Constitution, there has been relative peace and freedom for those who wish to preach God's Word and establish churches in this country. The favor toward churches has been as nurturing as the dew on the green grass in the springtime.

Family Discussion Questions:

1. What are some of the indications that a man is sinning in anger?

2. How can you explain the fact that Jesus' actions in the temple did not constitute sinful anger?

3. Is there ever a time when we must disobey the civil magistrate?

4. How has our country provided favor to those who love God and worship Him?

PART 146 ~ BLESSINGS AND CURSES FOR FAMILIES

Proverbs 19:13

A foolish son is the calamity of his father: and the contentions of a wife are a continual dropping.

We turn to the Bible for our ethical perspectives in life, which means that the Bible defines what is sinful and what is evil. Note that what is evil is not necessarily sinful. For example, contracting the measles is an evil thing, but it is not of itself sinful.

This verse gives us two evil things that will visit a family from time to time. First, a son who is easily taken by bad companions, falls into alcohol abuse and fornication, and sits around playing computer games instead of working at twenty years of age, is a curse and a shame to his father. The mere existence of this foolish son is an evil curse on his father. It is worse than the father contracting the measles. Yet, you may notice that the verse does not address the sin of it, or the cause of it. The son's foolishness is a consequence of many things, including his own rebellious heart. But the influence of ungodly peers, wicked cultural attractions, and the sinful abdication of a father's nurture could contribute as well. In our day especially, the hearts of fathers are badly separated from the hearts of their sons. But none of these things are mentioned in the verse, because every situation is unique. Rest assured that no matter how a son becomes foolish, he will be a sorrow, a calamity, a heaviness, and a lifelong disappointment to his father. That is the plain meaning of this text.

But secondly, the family is also cursed by a wife who gives way to the sin of contentiousness and complaining. Because a wife plays the part of a helper to complete her husband, she can either make or break him. Most husbands do not enjoy being in the presence of a wife who nags and complains and for those ungodly husbands who do not have the gumption to survive the marriage, they will quickly file divorce papers. Here Proverbs compares the nagging wife to something akin to Chinese water torture. She is relentless in her discontent, and she cannot restrain herself from airing her complaints to those who are closest to her.

While much of the Book of Proverbs is directed toward sons, this verse has an important lesson specifically intended for young women. They should be particularly wary of sins of the tongue. It is incumbent upon fathers who love their daughters and their future sons-in-law to work with their daughters in this area when they are young. Should our daughters attempt to manipulate others by sour attitudes, complain against the providence of God, or fail to express gratitude to God in the home, fathers must lovingly and patiently correct them for these things. Otherwise, our daughters will make lousy wives and miserable homes for the next generation. Whiny, bossy, nagging, ungrateful little girls will not make for loving, submissive wives and mothers. May God have mercy on our homes!

Proverbs 19:14

House and riches are the inheritance of fathers: and a prudent wife is from the LORD.

In contrast with the previous verse, this text provides two of God's blessings for families. Normatively, a good man passes an inheritance on to his children and to his grandchildren. This can be and has been severely curtailed by several generations that have consumed previous capital and then increased debt tenfold (per household, adjusted for inflation) since 1900. Inheritance can also be undermined by the devastation of war. But those countries that are blessed with moral integrity within and peace from without should see families passing on an inheritance to future generations. Sad to say, barely 5% of the present generation in this country will receive anything substantial from their parents in an inheritance.

The second blessing mentioned here is "a prudent wife." In contrast with the dripping faucet of the previous verse, this is a gifted, productive wife who can manage a home and see to the success of the household. The word "prudent" speaks of "know-how." In our vernacular, we would say that she is competent, skillful, and successful. When Dr. Thomas Stanley interviewed 722 millionaires in America and determined that the majority considered "a supportive spouse" an essential factor of success, he was only confirming the principle recorded by this wise sage 3,500 years earlier. So much of a man's success in life, whether it be in raising his children or managing his household affairs, rests upon the character of the wife he chooses to marry. Will she be a dripping faucet or a competent, hard-working, faithful, and prudent wife?

Family Discussion Questions:

1. How might we avoid becoming a curse to our family (as fathers, mothers, sons, and daughters)?

2. What is a "prudent" wife? How might our daughters aspire to become that faithful, prudent wife?

3. How might we break ranks with what is happening in the world and provide a good inheritance to our children and grandchildren? Does an inheritance include anything more than houses and riches?

PART 147 ~ THE DANGERS OF SLOTH AND NEGLIGENCE
Proverbs 19:15

Slothfulness casts into a deep sleep; and an idle soul shall suffer hunger.

When a young man is controlled by slothfulness, it is as if he has fallen under a spell. In our day, this slothfulness is characterized by the young teen who is addicted to computer games. When he is away from his games, he walks around in a dream-like state. He finds work boring and unfulfilling, because he has learned to live his life in a fantasy world. Sadly, there are millions of young men and some young women who will never wake up from their technology-enhanced stupor. Now some experts tell us that 70% of young men are not grown up by thirty years of age, and that ratio is up from 30% just forty years ago![3] Of course, our economies cannot survive this severe deprivation of character. For a time, children will live off the capital of previous generations, and then they will spend their children and grandchildren into debt (which has already happened in nations like America, Japan, and most of Europe). But then they will suffer hunger. Because of the many safety nets provided by socialist nanny states, it is hard for people to imagine the gnawing hunger pains they will experience when the nets break and economies collapse. Nevertheless, these truths cannot be denied or reasonably argued against. Without thorough repentance on a national level, we will no doubt see these truths enforced with a vengeance in our lifetimes. It's hard to imagine emaciated forms of starved men and women gripping their game controllers while economies collapse. But then we will understand that slothfulness casts into a deep sleep, and an idle soul shall suffer hunger.

Proverbs 19:16

He that keeps the commandment keeps his own soul; but he that despises his ways shall die.

When a family appreciates a pet, they will usually keep the pet. That means they will feed it, watch out for it, and be careful that it does not wander off. Should the pet dog be run over by a car in the road, the members of the household might be distraught for a few days or weeks. But most families don't turn every animal in the house into a pet. They do not pay much attention to the three mice that live in the basement. They

3 http://www.newsweek.com/2008/08/30/why-i-am-leaving-guyland.html

couldn't care less if the mice wandered off into some other home. In fact, they would prefer that! They do not "keep" the mice. The idea of "keeping" the commandment is to watch out for the commandment and be sure that it remains with us. Should a father keep the seventh commandment, he considers it important and relevant. If a father neglects to keep the seventh commandment, he will forget about it and probably abandon his wife and run around with other women. Hence, we would conclude that the seventh commandment is not important to him. This would be akin to a family that enjoyed a pet dog for five or six years, and then just forgot about it and let the thing wander off. Of course, this almost never happens with families who have grown fond of their pets. But you see that some people who remember to keep track of their pets often forget about the commandments of God.

Should a pet wander off, it is not uncommon for an entire family to trek around the surrounding neighborhood with posters in an effort to retrieve the wayward animal. But what if one of God's commandments should begin to fade away? What happens if things begin to slip in the household in respect to the use of God's name? Hopefully, there would be some urgency on the part of the head of the household to bring back the fear of God and respect for the Lord's name! He will go after the commandment if he has a special respect for the commandments of God. Keeping the commandments does not equate to sinless perfection because obedience can be a slippery thing. Pets wander and so do the commandments of God. But those who keep the commandments of God will go after those commandments when it is apparent that they are beginning to wander.

Now, if you are keeping track of the commandments of God, you will be keeping track of your own soul. When commandments wander, souls will wander, and every day hundreds of thousands of souls around the world wander into the yawning gates of hell. To ignore the commandments of God is to despise your own soul. But to love God is to love His commandments and to love your own soul.

Family Discussion Questions:

1. Does the temptation to slothfulness ever seep into our family? Will our children live off the capital of our generation, or will they add to it? How might they do this?

2. Do we keep an eye out for God's commandments ourselves? Which of the commandments seems to wander more than the rest? Are there some that we have ignored recently?

PART 148 ~ PITY FOR THE POOR AND YOUR SON
Proverbs 19:17

He that has pity on the poor lends to the LORD; and that which he has given will He pay him again.

God is very interested in the poor and the helpless. So when somebody else takes a special interest in the poor, God naturally takes note of it. In fact, this connection between Yahweh and the poor is so intimate that any kind of charity is taken as a loan to God Himself!

God always pays His loans. But do we infer from this that God will return every dollar we give in charity? Is this a one-for-one exchange? Actually, God is far more gracious than we are. Every day, He proves His grace to us by watering the earth and putting the food on our tables. He bestows mercy on the merciful (Matt. 5:6). Of course, mercy is not something that can be quantified or valued by a monetary metric.

This verse is a tremendous encouragement to the fellow who gives up his last one hundred dollars to help a poor brother pay his rent. It might be easy to worry about the future, while doing good in the present. On the other hand, this verse is not intended to feed our greed. One who reads a verse like this might be tempted to think that he will grow rich if he gives generously to charitable causes. That is not the intent of the verse.

Proverbs 19:18

Chasten your son while there is hope, and let not your soul spare for his
  crying.

Generally, people are not saved from their sins without being
exposed to the preaching of the Word; it's for the same reason
that seeds do not germinate and grow into plants without
being planted in the ground. This is not to say that every seed
planted will germinate and yield fruit. But planting seeds is
foundationally important if you are interested in producing
crops. Thus, planting seeds is a means by which germination
and growing take place. Likewise, sharing of the Word of
God, preaching of the Word of God, and the correcting and
chastising through God's Word are means of grace by which
germination and growing happen in the life of a child. Just
as planting seeds is God's assigned means for getting crops,
training a child according to the principles of God's Word
is God's assigned means of salvation for a child. Faithful,
consistent, loving, and patient discipline is how we bring our
children to God for salvation from their sins.

God has also ordained a window of opportunity in which
parents may reach their children's hearts with a message about
sin and the grace of God that saves from these sins. It is
incumbent on parents to take advantage of this opportunity.
We ought not to treat sin as "no big deal" by ignoring it or
by failing to correct it when we see it. If that is the message
our children receive, then they will have zero motivation to
cry out to God for His salvation from their sins. The pain
of sin corrected and the pain of conviction that comes by
direct preaching and rebuke is nothing in comparison to
the punishment God has instituted for sin. Godly discipline
should lead to repentance unto life because it points to the
transcendent law of God that was broken. When a child
understands the severity of his sins, he will begin to understand
the severity of the death of Jesus Christ on the cross.

What is presented here is not the father who strikes a child in impatient and self-centered anger for violating his own rules. This is rather the parent who, out of concern for the child's soul—and out of concern for the sanctity of God's holy law—is willing to patiently and consistently remind his child of these things.

Family Discussion Questions:

1. What part should God's promised rewards play in our minds when we make the decision to give something to the poor?

2. How do we view sin in our home? Is it a big deal? How do we view our own sins in comparison with the sins of others? How does a parent convey the seriousness of sin when he or she disciplines a child?

PART 149 ~ WISE COUNSEL
Proverbs 19:19

A man of great wrath shall suffer punishment: for if you deliver him, yet you must do it again.

There are men who get angry, and then there is the angry man who is characterized by that sin. Those poor souls that must interact with the angry man find themselves "walking on eggshells" so as not to irritate him to even the slightest degree. For if he is irritated, there is no telling what he will say or do. Inevitably, the angry man will suffer the consequences of his angry ways. When he loses his temper in the presence of a police officer, for example, he is remanded to the jail for "resisting arrest." When anger gets the better of him in the courtroom later, again he serves more time in prison for "contempt of the court." When his family or his friends intervene in an attempt to "fix" the problems he gets himself into, they find that they must do it again and again. They soon discover that it is better that he face the miserable consequences of his miserable habit than for them to get involved with him. Of course, this means that his family will suffer because of his foolish anger. Until the man repents of his anger problem in humility, it would be far better to minister in little ways to his family members than to minister to him.

Proverbs 19:20

Hear counsel, and receive instruction, that you may be wise in your latter end.

Some trees or plants that do not receive adequate water early in their growth cycle will fail to grow to full maturity and produce adequate fruit. Even if the plant is nurtured well later in its growth cycle, the plant languishes for lack of early care. It is therefore important that the plant receive the nourishing water and nutrients early on, that it might bear fruit a year or two later. The same principle applies to a young man or woman. Should a young man reject the wisdom provided to him in his early years, and should the soil of his heart be hard to the watering of the Word, he may very well find wisdom coming harder in his later years. What happens to those teenage rebels and scoffers who grow up in Christian homes with access to good wisdom and instruction but throw off those blessings? Generally, they will find wisdom harder to come by in their later years. This is not to say that they cannot pick up some wisdom later on, but it would have been so much better if they had received it in their younger years.

Proverbs 19:21

There are many devices in a man's heart; nevertheless the counsel of the LORD, that shall stand.

The *Humanist Manifesto* was a document issued by a group of highly influential leaders in this country shortly after the turn of the 20th century. These proud men wrote, "Man is at last becoming aware that he alone is responsible for the realization of the world of his dreams, that he has within himself the power for its achievement. He must set intelligence and will to the task."

The authors of this document really believed that man is in control of his own destiny. Whatever man would become by the year 2200 A.D. or 2500 A.D. would be entirely dependent upon the plans and intents of his own heart. Man's will, therefore, becomes the hinge point upon which reality swings. You must understand that this is the very heart and soul of humanism. Yet, the present text flatly contradicts such a metaphysical theory.

Never has man been more confident in his own planning. He really believes that he can predestine the future! Tens of thousands of bureaucrats plan the social conditions of the next generation through education funding in this country each year. They control the curriculum, the sexual behavior, the family size, the economic systems, and the political opinions of the next generation. The United Nations Population Fund issued its goals in the early part of the 21st century, aiming to end poverty in the world by the year 2015! Never in the history of the world has so much of the world's mass been controlled by large centralized governments. But all of this will come to nought!

"The LORD brings the counsel of the heathen to nought: He makes the devices of the people of none effect. The counsel of the LORD stands for ever, the thoughts of His heart to all generations."
Psalm 33:10–11

Men may make all the plans in the world, and those plans may come to fruition, or they may rot in the ash heap of history. But the wise plans, purposes, and counsels of our eternal, covenant-keeping God will always and forever stand.

There are many implications to such a basic metaphysical perspective of reality and history. When men reject the sovereignty of God in favor of the sovereignty of man, they reject an extremely basic biblical truth. Either God determines what will happen or man is the ultimate determinant, else we must leave it up to pure chance in a meaningless universe. Which will it be? We may plan to launch a successful business, or we may plan to bring a relative to a saving knowledge of Jesus Christ—and we may work diligently to those ends—but our success is always in the hands of God. It is His purpose that will stand! At the least this calls us to humility before God. For He can shift the direction of our lives, organizations, and empires any time He so desires. The founders of this country well understood this truth, as George Washington said in his memorable words at the Constitutional Convention: "Let us raise a standard to which the wise and the honest can repair. The event is in the hand of God."[4]

Family Discussion Questions:

1. How can anger ruin the life of a man (and his family)? What is an "angry man"? What can you do with an angry man?

2. Children, are your hearts soft to wisdom in your early years? Do you strive to understand the lessons that your parents teach you? Or are you bored, disinterested, and hard-hearted as you sit in family worship or in church?

3. Who is the ultimate determinant of what will happen in history?

4. When men believe that they control the future, what will they do with their governments? What do you think God thinks about this?

5. Do we trust in governments to determine the future for us, or are we trusting in God?

PART 150 ~ TWO BASICS—FEAR AND LOVE
Proverbs 19:22

The desire of a man is his kindness: and a poor man is better than a liar.

Above all things, the most commendable quality in a human being is kindness—undying, loyal love for others. If a man had courage, strength, and rhetorical abilities that could move entire nations, but had no love, he would be "nothing,"

4 William Peters, *A More Perfect Union* (New York: Crown Publishers, 1987)

according to the Apostle Paul (1 Cor. 13:1–2). Learn about love. Pray for love. Strive for love. In every opportunity you have to engage with others, find ways to deny yourself and give of yourself to others. By nature, we are a loveless bunch. Because there is no quality or commodity more desirable than love, let us strive to be more loving. Better to die penniless than to die loveless!

But secondly, it is also better to live a pauper than to prosper by lying. When men choose wealth as the chief end to which they will work and struggle and strive, they will compromise the truth every time. To gain wealth, they will sell their goods to people who do not need them. They will beat their competition by finding ways to surreptitiously remove value from the products they sell, while pretending to retain it. But at the end of the day, a man who sacrifices his integrity to gain wealth will eventually lose both.

Proverbs 19:23

The fear of the LORD tends to life: and he that has it shall abide satisfied; he shall not be visited with evil.

People are always motivated by some sort of fear. They may fear losing money, or they may fear losing their life, or they may fear offending others. Perhaps they fear the collapse of an empire more than they fear offending God. This is why men who refuse to fear the true and living God will resort to torture and "collateral damage" in their military campaigns. They will shoot up a village in order to obtain information on the whereabouts of some terrorist warlord who threatens to explode a nuclear weapon somewhere within the empire. The fear of men will cause men to overcompensate in their policies and actions. Because these people refuse to fear God, they create a hell on earth for themselves and for others. But this is not the life of men and nations whose God is the Lord! "When a man's ways please the Lord, He makes even his enemies to be at peace with him" (Prov. 16:7). When he fears God, he need fear nothing else!

If we could but learn to tremble in the presence of God as we view His powerful works in history, we would be as rooted as Mount Everest. We would not be the least concerned about the worst threats issuing from the very powers of hell, whether demons or men. The missionary John Paton was the subject of relentless attacks and constant physical threats to his life on the part of murderous, demonic savages during the years he spent on the island of Tanna in the South Seas. In his biography, he wrote concerning these deadly affairs, "At full speed a large body of the tallest and most powerful men that I had seen on Tanna came rushing on and filled the dancing ground. They were all armed and flushed with their success in war. . . they encircled us in a deadly ring, and one kept urging another to strike the first blow or fire the first shot. My heart rose up to the Lord Jesus; I saw Him watching all the scene. My peace came back to me like a wave from God. I realized that I was immortal till my Master's work with me was done. The assurance came to me as if a voice out of Heaven had spoken, that not a musket would be fired, without the permission of Jesus Christ whose is all power in Heaven and on Earth."[5]

Family Discussion Questions:

1. Do you desire to love others more? Do you desire love more than wealth? In what specific areas could you grow in love?

2. For what will you seek after in this life? Do you live and breathe to gain wealth, or are you seeking wisdom and building integrity into your life by every business transaction you engage in and by every relationship you cultivate?

3. Why was the missionary John Paton so courageous in the face of imminent death? How might you gain that kind of courage?

5 John Paton, *Missionary Patriarch: The True Story of John G. Paton* (San Antonio: Vision Forum, 2001)

PART 151 ~ SLOTHS AND SCOFFERS
Proverbs 19:24

A slothful man hides his hand in his bosom, and will not so much as bring it to his mouth again.

The sluggard is the man who is caught in the horrible condition of perpetual slothfulness. He is held down by velvet chains in a sea of cushions, and it has become almost impossible for him to extricate himself from this horrible predicament. Once a person is caught in the trap of slothfulness, he will find that every minor effort requires gargantuan willpower to accomplish. From Proverbs 26:13, we know that the sluggard is intimidated by lions in the street, and there may be real lions that prohibit him from getting his work done in the fields. But now that he is intimidated by the obstacle of lions, he soon finds it hard to distinguish between real lions and harmless kitty cats. Every responsibility becomes a burdensome task because he is a sluggard, and sluggards are intimidated by everything! Therefore this verse presents the awful scenario of a sluggard who considers basic tasks, such as feeding himself, an intolerable inconvenience!

A poor wretch like this does not turn into a sluggard overnight. When a little boy fails to make his bed for two hundred days despite his mother's constant reminders, or when he drags his feet every day when doing his chores, he works his way toward a life of slothfulness. If he will not repent of this sin, and if his parents continue to allow it in his life, he may be sentenced to the miserable existence of the sluggard for the rest of his life.

Proverbs 19:25

Strike a scoffer, and the simple will learn prudence; reprove a man of understanding, and he will gain knowledge. (ESV)

What does a family do with an incorrigible teenage rebel? Unfortunately, this question is common in counseling situations today, where families must deal with a generation of those who curse their fathers and whose teeth are as swords

(Prov. 30:11–14)! The civil magistrate tolerates these out-of-control youths, while at the same time it will not permit families to emancipate them. This puts families in a tight spot. Too often, these scoffers turn the home into a tumultuous, chaotic, miserable place, presenting a terrible influence to the rest of the children. There is only one thing to do: strike the scoffer. According to the important principle in the present verse, striking the scoffer will more than likely do nothing for the rebel himself. But the striking of the scoffer is not for his benefit because you must remember this young man is (at least for the time being) beyond correction. Rather it is for the benefit of all the other children around him. In a powerful object lesson, they witness the force of punishment. They see the hardness of heart, and they fear the curse of rebellion and sin! In short, they learn prudence.

Quite opposite to the scoffer, there is the young man of true wisdom and godly character. He will not need the rod, but he may need an occasional reproof. When he is reproved, he eagerly receives it for the wisdom he can find in it. Oftentimes, a reproof may not identify the true problems with perfect accuracy. Yet a man of understanding will still carefully examine the reproof for the wisdom he can find in it. It may be that the criticism was somewhat misdirected, but he does find in it a kernel of truth that pointed to another problem of far more relevance and import. You can see that it takes a humble heart to carefully consider any critical feedback directed toward him.

Family Discussion Questions:

1. Is the slothful bug growing on you right now? Are you faithful in performing the simple tasks around the house? What sort of jobs do you perceive to be too difficult? Do you drag your feet at certain challenges? Give examples.

2. What is the best way to overcome slothfulness?

3. Why would a parent strike a scoffer (or a "teenage rebel")?

PART 152 ~ WICKED SONS AND UNGODLY TEACHERS
Proverbs 19:26

He that wastes his father, and chases away his mother, is a son that causes shame, and brings reproach.

Here and there, you will find parents who are afraid of their son. Chances are that the rebellion began when he was nine years old. His rebellion was ten times worse in his tenth year, and ten times worse again in his eleventh year, and so on. It would take your breath away if you saw the extent to which a man may rebel, dishonor his parents, and engage in violence toward others.

As a police officer pulls over some young man on the highway for speeding, what would you say if the young man were to pull out a .22 rifle and start taking pot shots at the officer? You would have to conclude that he has little respect for the officer—and certainly no fear of the power of the state, the courts, the prison systems, and the entire police force of that jurisdictional authority! Likewise, a young man who refuses to honor his father and mother has little or no respect for the God Who deputized those parents and demanded honor for His deputies. If a man refuses to honor God and his own parents, it is doubtful that he will honor anybody else. He is, in the true sense of the term, a dangerous man.

One Sunday morning, on December 7, 2007, a young man killed five people in a murderous rampage across the state of Colorado. But months before this happened, the same young man issued a post on his web site bearing some of the most hateful and vile curses ever recorded toward his Christian parents. A man's relationship with his own parents is a good gauge by which to assess his relationships in other social contexts. A man who curses his father and has earned the severe disfavor of his mother will one day doubtless find his mug shot prominently displayed in a regional news outlet.

Proverbs 19:27

Cease, my son, to hear the instruction that causes to err from the words of knowledge.

If the beginning of knowledge is the fear of God, what would you do if you came across somebody who was trying to teach a form of knowledge divorced from the acknowledgement of God? What would you do if somebody was trying to teach history without any recognition of God whatsoever? Or what should you do if some university professor was trying to teach chemistry without trembling a little before the God Who created chemistry? If you were to accept Proverbs 1:7 as having anything to say about knowledge, it seems that this is a man who is not qualified to teach true knowledge. The good father here warns his son not to sit at the feet of an instructor who would cause his students to err from the path of true knowledge.

For many centuries, Christian parents considered education as those things taught by the intellectuals—the pagan Greeks, the transcendentalists, the Unitarians, and other humanists. So they gave their children books written by the great humanist thinkers. In this way, they set their children at the feet of the greatest humanist writers, thinkers, and teachers. Then, they were surprised when their children rebelled against the faith through the 19th and 20th centuries. As millions of professing Christians in Europe and America sent their children to humanist high schools and colleges, they couldn't understand why their children turned out to be homosexuals like Walt Whitman, socialists like Karl Marx, or godless evolutionists like Charles Darwin. Of course, they chose the wrong teachers, the wrong schools, and the wrong textbooks for their children! How tragic it is to think of the hundreds of millions of children in public schools, private schools, and home schools who turned away from the faith through the generations because their teachers in the classrooms (and in the textbooks) were intellectuals who refused to conform their thinking to a biblical worldview. It would have been far better if they had heeded the words of this little Proverb, "Cease my son, to hear the instruction that causes to err from the words of knowledge!"

Family Discussion Questions:

1. How is the honor of parents tied into the honor of the civil magistrate?

2. What would be the signs that one of our children was beginning to walk down the path toward rebellion?

3. In what ways might a young man be taught by those who do not fear the true and living God (in our day)?

4. Name some people who have rejected the truth of Scripture and have written the "great literature" that is used by humanist schools today.

PART 153 ~ DANGEROUS FOOLS
Proverbs 19:28

An ungodly witness scorns judgment: and the mouth of the wicked devours iniquity.

There are men in this world who will take nothing seriously because they will not take God seriously. As evidence that they refuse to fear God, they see little importance in anything they do in their lives. Eventually, these turn into dangerous men. They feel they can do anything without suffering any consequences. Generally, men like this are the ones who rob liquor stores in the slums of New York, but more often today, they go to college and get advanced degrees. And the destruction they bring upon society is far greater than the thug who takes down liquor stores. One of these characters shows up in Fyodor Dostoyevski's famous book, *The Brothers Karamazov*. Assuming there is no God, the young man, Ivan, concludes that "Everything is permitted." One would shudder to think of what Ivan might do if he began to act on that premise! Would you want this man to serve as a witness in a murder trial, for example? Would he come down on the side of what is right and true? When such men serve in positions of responsibility in the government bureaucracy, social services departments, or the judicial arena, justice becomes a haphazard affair. In the end, this man scorns judgment because he doesn't take God's law seriously and doesn't take God seriously.

The verse gives us more insight into the life of the wicked. As a rule, wicked men get worse and worse over time. They turn on the faucet of evil and gulp down everything they can get. Even as a moth can't help but fly into the flame, their hearts are drawn to evil. What holds them back from being as evil as they could be and becoming destructive to themselves and to others? Sometimes the restraints of whatever righteous civil government is left in a society can prevent them from playing out their evil intentions. But the only thing that will stop them from their strong draw toward evil is a change of heart.

Proverbs 19:29

Judgments are prepared for scorners, and stripes for the back of fools.

Those who live quiet and peaceable lives and those who honor their parents and the civil magistrate will generally not run into problems in a well-run society. This is the thrust of passages like Romans 13:1–8. But those young fools who refuse to honor their parents and think nothing of firing a rifle at a police vehicle will run into the most trouble with the law.

For a time, young rebels may get away with their refusal to obey their parents. They may enjoy slothful lifestyles where they live off the good graces of others, and they may appear to do well for a while with their well-to-do, decadent lifestyles. But as the years go by, they will find themselves without jobs, sloughing along with the dregs of humanity. At one time in history, men were reduced to slavery and beatings if they refused to work. Today, they live with women on welfare until they are arrested for drug possession or petty criminal activity. Then, they serve time in slave camps called "prisons." It is interesting that a nation like America who prides itself for its "freedom" maintains the highest incarceration rate in the world. Without character, and without a willingness to honor authority and work hard, men will inevitably subject themselves to prisons and sound beatings (either from the magistrate or a slave owner—or even other ruffians with whom they associate).

Family Discussion Questions:

1. Why would it be a risk to put a man on the witness stand who didn't fear God?

2. What happens to wicked men over time?

3. What happens to men who refuse to work in this country or other countries?

PART 154 ~ THE ALCOHOL TRAP
Proverbs 20:1

Wine is a mocker, strong drink is raging: and whoever is deceived thereby is not wise.

The social consequences of alcohol abuse around the world are immeasurable. Over thousands of years, the abuse of alcohol and drugs has brought unspeakable misery to untold billions of people. For example, the number of children born with fetal alcohol syndrome has exploded in recent years, and it is now the "leading known cause for mental retardation." Between 40% and 60% of automobile accident fatalities are alcohol-related. Child abuse, family disintegration, economic distress, and deleterious health conditions are just a few other sad consequences of this cursed sin. Recently, nations like Russia have faced drunkenness at epidemic proportions, where the average man or woman drinks a quart of vodka every week. Incredibly, some of its cities have lost a quarter of their populations to alcohol-related illnesses and accidents over just the last fifteen years!

Outfitted with attractive labeling like "Southern Comfort," a bottle of hard whiskey lures the hapless victim in for the kill. The first sip seems to provide a little comfort, so why not a second? As soon as the poor wretch embraces the bottle, it then proceeds to beat him senseless. Promised more sweet comfort the following day, the drunkard swallows the hook again, only to repeat the same process. Thus, alcohol always promises something that it cannot deliver. Those who are deceived by it will eventually find their families in shambles, their children suffering from fetal alcohol syndrome, and their bodies ravaged by cirrhosis of the liver and other diseases. Often this sin of drunkenness leaves a generational curse on a man's children and grandchildren. The sad stories told of Noah and Lot in their drunkenness remind us of how incredibly damaging this sin can be—as it opens the door for the visitation of other sins and curses upon future generations.

Hard liquor is raging like a storm. It has the potential to do much damage, especially if it is ingested by a human being in large quantities. Alcohol is also a deceiver, and in this sense it can be dangerous. But so is parachuting out of an airplane or rappelling down sheer mountain cliffs. Obviously, one must be very careful when feeding lions in the zoo or swimming with sharks. Even the most accomplished lion tamers have been mauled by their big cat "friends." While Paul does remind us that "all things are lawful," this is not to say that all things are equally "safe" and "profitable."

Proverbs 20:2

The fear of a king is as the roaring of a lion: whoso provokes him to anger sins against his own soul.

Christians are counter-cultural. When we bring the Gospel to a foreign country, it is important that we do not go out of our way to pick a fight with the government. While He was here, Jesus paid His tax to the authorities at the time, "lest we offend them." Paul encourages us to, as much as lies in us, live at peace with all men. Yet, both Jesus and Paul were executed by the Roman magistrate. For a time, we may be able to "fly under the radar" as we attempt to replace the kingdoms of the devil with the kingdom of God. Indeed it is a delicate game to play. It would be easier to avoid confrontation altogether, but God calls us to disciple the nations. Should a household, a city, or a nation utterly refuse to hear the Gospel, it may be better to leave and take the message elsewhere, where it would be better received. These verses are placed here to give us wisdom as we interact with the world around us.

For related commentary, reference Proverbs 16:14 and Proverbs 19:12.

Family Discussion Questions:

1. Describe the sort of destruction that alcohol can bring to a family or to a society. Would it be better to stay out of the lions' cages altogether? Would it be better to stay away from alcohol entirely (except for medicinal purposes, cleaning purposes, etc.)?

2. How can we best maintain a friendly relationship with our governments without compromising our message?

PART 155 ~ HOW TO DEAL WITH STRIFE
Proverbs 20:3

It is an honor for a man to cease from strife: but every fool will be meddling.

Strife is evil. As cancer and auto accidents are evil, so strife is evil. Though not necessarily sinful, these evil consequences are practically inevitable in a sinful world. But how must we deal with evil? Of course, medical doctors seek to relieve the evil of disease and suffering, and we must do our level best to bring strife to an end wherever it occurs.

Strife seems to be as inevitable in this world of sin as the curse of sickness and pain. Thus all of us should strive to be peacemakers, working our way out of the labyrinth of each conflict in which we happen to find ourselves. There are many ways in which to work through conflicts. Unfortunately, it is rare to find truly honorable men who have the character, the desire, and the wisdom to bring conflicts to an end. But this is what we must learn to do. Here are several ways in which conflicts are brought to an end.

1. *Stop talking.* In the multitude of words there is no lack of sin, and gossip always fans the flames of conflict.

2. *Confess your own sins, and ask for forgiveness.* Often this is a good way to bring conflict to a quick end.

3. *Submit to the counsel of reconcilers.* Those who love strife will hate the idea of reconciliation, and by this they prove their hatred for God. But if there are disagreements in the family, children should quickly submit to the counsel of their parents, accept the consequences for their behavior, confess the sins that were raised in the counsel, and work to restore relationships.

4. *A gift in secret may appease wrath.* Although not usually effective at resolving deep-rooted conflicts, it is something that can soften the heart of your enemy.

5. *You might also let yourself be defrauded to some degree, especially if the things being argued about are minor.* You must be careful not to lend support to your brother's sins. But if his sins are unclear, and your relationship is such that you cannot clearly understand his issues, then it's always best to err on the side of letting yourself be defrauded.

6. *Separate the protagonists.* Occasionally, church communities are plagued by a divisive, schismatic person, but proper church discipline should result in the separation of these troublemakers from the flock (Prov. 26:20; Titus 3:10).

One way or another, we must take active steps to bring strife to an end. We cannot allow it to continue indefinitely, or it will destroy our families and communities.

Then, in contrast to the honorable man is the fool who sees no need to put an end to the strife. In fact, he revels in the strife.

For some reason, he cannot understand the fact that there is no profit in the strife itself. But the reality is that there is only profit in *working a way out of strife!* If, after some counsel with those with whom you strive, you conclude that one or both of the protagonists have no desire to end the strife, you have to conclude that you are dealing with fools.

Proverbs 20:4

The sluggard will not plow by reason of the cold; therefore shall he beg in harvest, and have nothing.

There is always a reason why the sluggard cannot do his work. In all of his years of sluggishness, this young man has learned to do one thing exceptionally well—come up with creative excuses as to why he didn't do what he was supposed to. So he will starve to death along with all of his excuses.

But we will teach our sons responsibility. They must learn that responsible people do not make excuses. Responsible people take responsibility for their mistakes. When they are given responsibilities, they make sure they're done. They double-check their work to make sure that it was done completely and they met or exceeded expectations. If a mother expects the bed to be made each day, the child will make the bed and do it to his mother's expectations. (Of course, parents must be careful not to place unreasonable expectations on their children and thereby provoke them to wrath.)

Obstacles are not excuses for us. They only force us to work harder and more creatively in order to overcome them. We must resolve in our minds that our dominion work will always entail obstacles, and it will be by the sweat of our brow that we will bring forth fruit out of this land. Without this mindset, people starve to death. Those who procrastinate and fail to sow seeds in the present will not reap in the future.

Family Discussion Questions:

1. What is the difference between strife and evil things like cancer and auto accidents?

2. What are some good ways to bring conflict to an end?

3. What would you do with a person who persists in continuing a conflict with another, refusing to do anything to resolve it?

4. Think of a certain project that you have worked on recently. What sort of obstacles did you confront, and how did you overcome them? Were you discouraged by the obstacles or more driven to overcome them?

PART 156 ~ FINDING WISE MEN AND FAITHFUL FRIENDS
Proverbs 20:5

Counsel in the heart of man is like deep water; but a man of understanding will draw it out.

The best gems are usually the hardest to obtain. You won't find them lying on the surface of the ground. Yet these precious stones are valuable and highly desirable, so men will invest great amounts of capital and time to dig them out. How much more valuable, then, are the gems of wisdom? To properly discern the challenges we face in life and the biblical solutions that we must bring to them is the secret to success in life. If we desire to be successful at leading our families, establishing godly churches, and running successful businesses, we must apply sound wisdom. But where do we get good wisdom? How do we make proper assessments of problems—whether they are behavioral problems in people or technical issues in our dominion work? Certainly, it would be convenient to diagnose every problem with some little manual, complete with a nice comprehensive index! But life is far more complicated than that, and every situation requires its own analysis and the careful application of wisdom.

Most of the time, the kind of wisdom that we need is hidden deep in the minds of others. In fact, these folks may not even be aware that they have the wisdom needed for the present challenges facing the family or the church. So first, we must acknowledge that others have wisdom that we do not have. It is for us to dig. However, as it turns out, those who have the most wisdom are also the ones who are "swift to hear, slow to speak, and slow to anger!" (James 1:19) As the old saying goes, "Still waters run deep," and these folks are not always overly munificent with their wisdom. So a man of understanding will seek to dig deeper into that man's well of knowledge by thoughtful, creative questions. Asking questions of others is one of the most powerful ways to draw knowledge from the deep wells accessible to us!

Proverbs 20:6

Most men will proclaim everyone his own goodness: but a faithful man who can find?

It is rare to find a man who honestly thinks himself an unfaithful, disloyal, miserable wretch! As a matter of fact, most people think that they make pretty decent friends. When conflicts occur in relationships, it is rather uncommon for either of the parties to consider themselves as the truly self-centered, treacherous party in the melee. Truth be told, the vast majority of people in this world make for pretty lousy friends. They are easily embittered against their own brothers and sisters, husbands and wives. They offend others and are painfully slow to confess those sins. This is the sad state of relationships in a fallen world. But as the Spirit of God begins to move in the hearts of those who have been visited by the steadfast, die-hard covenantal love of God Himself, things begin to change. Eventually, you will find friends who are willing to go to the mat for you. You find friends who would die for you because they had a Friend Who once died for them!

Family Discussion Questions:

1. Do you look at other people as virtual wells of knowledge from which you might draw something good and helpful? What sorts of questions might you ask in order to draw something out of somebody?

2. What is the state of relationships in our world? Is divorce common in our communities? Do we cultivate long-term, die-hard friendships? Are you a faithful friend?

PART 157 ~ AUTHENTIC MEN AND RIGHTEOUS JUDGES
Proverbs 20:7

The just man walks in his integrity: his children are blessed after him.

Of all the fatal flaws in "Christian" families, none are so deadly as false authenticity and hypocrisy. For a time, some families may talk a good talk and pretend to aspire to biblical standards in theology, education, dress, music, church involvement, economics, and evangelism. However, time is the great revealer. Eventually, those facades always wear thin, and the true condition of the heart becomes evident for all to see. When all the filth of the heart pours out, everyone around them will know that they pretended to be something they were not. Ananias and Saphira piously claimed to have given the entire price of their holdings to the church, but it turned out that they lied. They presented themselves as something more than what they were. So God killed them (Acts 5:1–5). He is merciful to sinners, but he will not tolerate fakes. May God help us to walk in our integrity! This does not imply a sinless perfection. No, rather it is a humble and contrite assessment of ourselves and a life that comports with our profession. As the Apostle Paul tells the Ephesian brothers, "I therefore, the prisoner of the Lord, beseech you that you walk worthy of the vocation wherewith you are called" (Eph. 4:1).

How then does this apply to a family? Occasionally, you will find a "Christian" father who persistently tries to hold his children to standards he would never hold to himself. He may speak strongly about family values and then proceed to divorce his own wife. He opposes abortion, but his relationships with his own children are in terrible shape. He demands obedience of his own children, but he has never really submitted himself to the elders in the church in any meaningful way. It won't be long before this man's children get the message. Hypocrisy is the name of the game. If Father lives his life as a hypocrite, why shouldn't they? Or they may condemn their father's hypocrisy and embrace full-fledged, all-out rebellion against God, the church, and the Word the family pretended to profess. Sadly, this has been very much the legacy of the Christian faith in this country since the 1950s, during the great Western apostasy of the 20th and 21st centuries.

Thankfully, there is still a faithful man here and there who walks in his integrity! This man utterly repudiates hypocrisy and purges it from his own life wherever he finds it. He truly submits to the counsel of his elders to whom he is accountable. He humbly confesses his sin before his family when he sins against them. In his case, the man on the outside is the man on the inside, and he is a true man who loves His God and seeks to serve Him. And his children see it! By God's blessing, his children will walk in God's ways and be blessed!

Proverbs 20:8

A king that sits in the throne of judgment scatters away all evil with his eyes.

When John G. Paton, the great missionary of the 19th century, visited the heathen in the islands of the New Hebrides for the first time, he found the chaos of cannibalism, constant war, theft, kidnapping, and murder everywhere. From his first-hand reports, we learned that the first worship services were fairly chaotic, with the clucking of hens and the squealing of pigs everywhere. This is because the natives felt compelled to bring all of their personal belongings, including their animals, with them to the meetings for fear that their things would be stolen if they left them at home. You must remember that these islands were untouched by the influence of the Christian and Jewish law systems for thousands of years (unlike Europe, Russia, India, and China), and they had no understanding of biblical justice. As the Gospel penetrated these distant islands, court systems based on biblical law were put in place, securing the property and persons of those living on the islands. So eventually, the chickens and pigs stayed safely at home while the worship services took place!

Consider the great blessing of kings or judges that sit in the seats of judgment, whether they be in the South Sea islands of the New Hebrides or in your particular county. You do not have to live in constant fear that your property or life will be unjustly taken from you. In some places in this country, families feel comfortable leaving their homes unlocked as they take their vacations. This is for two reasons: there is still some respect for the power of the courts, and there is some just use of the power of the courts in those vicinities.

Family Discussion Questions:

1. Do we live a life that comports with our profession? Or are we hiding some sin that grossly contradicts what we have professed to others? Give examples of how we might hold others to standards we do not hold to ourselves.

2. How safe is our city or county, in comparison to the New Hebrides? Is it safe to leave our doors unlocked at night? To what extent are the courts legislating and enforcing just laws against murder and theft (according to God's laws) where we live? Do young men in our city or county really respect the power of the judges and police?

PART 158 ~ SINLESS PERFECTION—IMPOSSIBLE
Proverbs 20:9

Who can say, I have made my heart clean, I am pure from my sin?

Of all the short, pithy statements we have studied thus far in the Proverbs, this little gem may be the most potent! It draws away the veil from the human heart and points to man's basic problem—the problem of sin. It is a universal problem.

Yet the Book of Proverbs repeatedly commends the righteous for their integrity, truth, and wisdom. If this be the case, can we say that these righteous men have made their own hearts clean and pure of all sin? Because all of us are contaminated with the curse of sin, there is no man on the earth who has cleansed his own heart from sin. How then may one be righteous if he is unable to cleanse his own heart? The answer is obvious to the man who cries out with the Psalmist, "Cleanse me with hyssop and I shall be clean, wash me and I shall be whiter than snow!" (Ps. 51:3–5) Whether he be an Old or New Testament saint, every one of us is only cleansed if God Himself does the cleansing. We know that this can only happen by the blood sacrifice of Jesus Christ on the cross.

Proverbs 20:10

Divers weights, and divers measures, both of them are alike abomination to the LORD.

Governments have corrupted themselves many times by issuing money with little or no intrinsic value. In 36 B.C., Marc Anthony first introduced the copper coin gilt with silver as a means of monetary exchange. Octavian, or Augustus Caesar, restored a solid silver denarii and solidified his rule over the empire. But gradually the Roman government gave way to debasement of the money supply, and this contributed to the breakdown of Rome. Interestingly, the Byzantium kingdom lasted much longer, largely because it committed to a system of hard money. When a copper coin is covered with a thin layer of silver, people are led to believe that it is worth more than it is. This is what happens with our systems of paper money as well. People believe that it is worth more than paper. At first, there may have been a silver backing for the paper money. But gradually the paper money is devalued, until people learn that it is worth nothing more than…well, paper.

God is vitally concerned with the exchange of goods and services that occurs in stores, through catalog orders, or over the Internet all over the world. When men intentionally and knowingly change the value of a commodity or monetary instrument in a trade, they commit this abomination. Dishonesty can be systemic and corporate, or it can be individual. Even though men may come together in corporations, banking systems, and governments to break God's law, this does not excuse their sin. They may hide behind their corporations and banking systems, assuming that the institutionalization of their sinful practices will exonerate them in the Day of Judgment. But they only deceive themselves. While looking down on a petty apple merchant that cheats his customer in some no-account market in South America, they glory in their fractionalized banking systems. As these banking systems collude with governments, they serve to reward certain large debtors, centralize power, and enslave the masses. After one hundred years, the average household is saddled with twenty times more debt (adjusted for inflation) than it was a hundred years ago. By inflating the money supply (and reducing the value of money used for trade), these modern bankers encouraged millions of people into debt—slavery which inevitably leads toward more government-based slavery.

Family Discussion Questions:

1. What is man's basic problem?

2. Who can clean our hearts?

3. How did the Romans in the old Roman Empire debase their money used for trade?

4. How did the bankers encourage millions of people into debt slavery?

Part 159 ~ THE CONDITION OF THE HEART REVEALED

Proverbs 20:11

Even a child is known by his doings, whether his work be pure, and whether it be right.

The true character of the heart is always revealed by the manner of life one lives. Although people learn quickly how to maintain thin facades over their wicked hearts, those who live with them for a year or two will see through them. Young children, however, are not as accomplished in the hypocrisy game. Therefore, you do not need to live with them for a year before you discern the true condition of their hearts. Usually within thirty minutes or so, you will see their self-centeredness, pride, envy, and covetousness prominently displayed.

In fact, much of our child training teaches children to construct facades. They quickly learn to suppress their true intentions, especially if they want to avoid the pain of punishment or disapprobation. Even, compliant children may quietly restrain their rebellion until a more convenient time. When they come of age, they then cast off their parent's good counsel and restraints in order to live riotous, ungodly lives. This transformation usually comes as a tremendous surprise to those who thought they knew the once well-behaved, demure youngster. "She used to be such a good kid, but now look at her!" is usually what they say.

But then there is also the "special needs" child who wears his heart inside out for all to see. For some reason, he is incapable of concealing the wickedness of his heart, and the rod seems of little use to either form the protective facades over his heart or to produce any substantial change of heart. Much of the immediate change that comes by the use of the rod is only external. It does make it easier to live with most children (when it is used properly). So as we apply both the rod of correction and the rod of the Word over many years, we must trust that God will work His heart-level change in the child, whether he be a special-needs child or not.

Proverbs 20:12

The hearing ear, and the seeing eye, the LORD has made even both of them.

How might we know the truth about the world, about ourselves, and about the God Who made us? It is by the complex design of the eye and the ear that we learn truth. Our capacity to take in information from the world around us and to process it is all part of the creation of God. With the exception of a few people who can neither hear nor see, we all hear the words of truth by out ears, or see them as our eyes scan the pages of books or witness events taking place around us.

This assertion should at least confirm for us our dependence upon God for everything. We are not gods. We have not created ourselves, nor have we provided ourselves with the capacity to perceive or understand the truth. And once we have eyes and ears, we still may not correctly grasp the truth. There are plenty of men with eyes and ears who are entirely deceived about the world, themselves, and the nature of God. In the words of the Apostle, their minds are blinded, "lest the light of the glorious Gospel of Christ, Who is the image of God, should shine unto them" (2 Cor. 4:3–4). Again, it must be God Who gives us ears to hear and eyes to see if the light of the glorious Gospel will shine into our dark souls!

Family Discussion Questions:

1. How can we tell that a child is being self-centered or proud? What are the sorts of things he might do or say?

2. How do children construct their facades?

3. How do we come to the knowledge of truth?

PART 160 ~ SUCCESS IN ECONOMICS
Proverbs 20:13

Love not sleep, lest you come to poverty; open your eyes, and you shall be satisfied with bread.

Young men in particular are given to the sin of slothfulness, and one strong indication that we have a problem of laziness on our hands is a love of sleep. Does the young man get out of bed on his own, or does he need the insistent prodding of his mother or father to get him up and moving in the morning?

Perhaps the worst cases of this form of slothfulness are found with young men who have no responsibility to attend a school or college, no regular employment, no farm animals to feed, and no urgency to get anything done on any given day. Add to that passive parents who tend to their every need, and you have a disaster on your hands. Either they are in love with their escapist pastimes in the electronic world (which is a sort of sleep state), or they will burn daylight each morning by sleeping in until 10:00 a.m.

The first step, therefore, toward success in life and overcoming the sin of laziness is to get out of bed! Until and unless a young man is able to get up and out of bed on his own, he is destined to live a life of poverty. Every day, we must get up and get about productive labor, whether or not we are paid for it. This goes for eight-year-old children as well as eighteen-year-old men and women.

The incredible failure of our economies in the 21st century and the breakdown of character among the youth are directly tied to the child labor laws and the mistaken notion that children should not be employed early on within the household economy. Of course, the systemic abuses in child labor occurred when families turned their children over to the corporations. So throughout the 1800s, children were passed on to the state by means of compulsory school attendance laws. It was only a matter of time before these family-fragmenting socio-economic systems would fail, namely, because the integrity of the family folded. There was very little meaningful work for many young men and women in the home. Fathers and mothers had far fewer opportunities to train their children to work in a trade and participate in family economies. In one way or another, we must revive family economies and train our children in work from an early age. If they learn to enjoy the challenges and the rewards of work, they will eagerly anticipate getting out of bed on Monday morning to address themselves to their labors.

Proverbs 20:14

It is naught, it is naught, says the buyer: but when he is gone his way, then he boasts.

Some societies are far more dishonest than others, and this always impoverishes the nation as a whole. An organization called Transparency International performs an honesty survey each year and finds the most dishonest nations are typically Muslim, Communist, and Roman Catholic—and they are desperately poor. Of the ten most honest nations in the world, the majority have their roots in the Protestant Reformation, and, of course, they enjoy more economic freedom and a good deal more prosperity. Another organization purposefully dropped hundreds of wallets containing cash in various nations all around the world, finding similar results. Again, the dishonest nations refused to return the lost wallets, clearly violating of the law of God (Deut. 5:19).

When tradesmen are perpetually controlled by their immediate self-interest and give way to dishonesty in their haggling, they actually foster a system of mistrust, inefficiency, and robbery. A spirit of dishonesty hampers trade. When a buyer realizes that he paid too much for a product or service, he will be less interested in engaging in more trade in that system. If he has been burned once, he will think twice before shopping at the same market.

In this case, it is the buyer who takes advantage of an unwary seller. Perhaps he buys a car from a widow who has no idea how to research car prices in the *Blue Book*. She doesn't understand the value of the car, and he quickly figures out that he can easily shave $2,000 off of the value of a $12,000 vehicle. After all, she may never find out that she was robbed. Of course, he doesn't want to reveal the fact that he is getting a really great deal for the car, so he acts as if he is breaking the bank to make the deal happen. He lies in a careful and discrete manner. But it is still a lie, and every lie breaks down his character and erodes the integrity of the market. It is these flaws in character that impoverish a nation. Should you notice that a check-out clerk failed to charge you for an item in your shopping cart, it is easy to ignore the matter and quietly walk away. But these are the everyday decisions that make you who you are. Should you habitually take the wrong approach as you engage in trade, you will undermine the integrity of our "free" markets.

Family Discussion Questions:

1. What is the first step toward success in life?

2. Why did the government introduce child labor laws and compulsory attendance laws in the 19th century?

3. Why does the buyer say, "It is nothing! It is nothing!"?

4. What happens to an economy when people refuse to return lost wallets or when they are under-charged for an item and refuse to disclose it?

PART 161 ～ HONESTY IN TEACHING AND BUSINESS

Proverbs 20:15

There is gold, and a multitude of rubies: but the lips of knowledge are a precious jewel.

This verse speaks of the rarity of wise teaching. Sadly, the world is filled with a cacophony of voices that provide every imaginable strain of falsehood. Libraries and bookstores are filled with all the forms of deceitful and foolish notions ever concocted in the wayward hearts of men. God communicates His wisdom in Scripture, yet men quickly wander from these truths, as evidenced by the Christian and Jewish apostasies that have risen over the last several millennia. When you find a man who roots his thinking in God's inspired revelation, and he communicates this truth in fear and humility, this is a rare gift indeed. May God raise up these men to preach in our communities of brothers and sisters in the years to come!

Proverbs 20:16

Take his garment that is surety for a stranger: and take a pledge of him for a strange woman.

Previously, in the Proverbs the wise father warns his son to avoid making contracts involving long term commitments with strangers—that is, people with whom he has not lived in community with for an extended period of time. Unfortunately, most developed countries with cities exceeding a population of 100,000 are filled with strangers who hardly know each other. They move from place to place, and they take their reputations with them. It is as if we have become nations filled with gypsies and nomads. Yet the gypsies and nomads travelled as clans and maintained communities on the road. This is hardly the case with many of our people in modern cities today.

Now, here the book of wisdom takes this principle one step further, cautioning us to be careful with those who make it a habit to contract with strangers. At the very least, if we are to do business in this sort of a market (where almost everybody is in "bed" with strangers), we should be sure to hold some collateral for the loans. The current financial systems serve as prime examples of what happens when strangers do business with strangers and there is no meaningful collateral for the debts. People walk away from their mortgaged properties on a regular basis, taking whatever other assets they have with them. Within a few years their credit ratings are such that they will secure more debt, and once again they can live beyond their means on somebody else's dime. The banks claim bankruptcy, and the taxpayers inevitably pay for the losses insured by the government's deposit insurance programs. Unfortunately, all of us are bound up in this system where nobody feels accountable to anybody, and should the modern systems of finance collapse, all of us will pay dearly for it.

For related commentary, reference Proverbs 6:1 and Proverbs 11:5.

Proverbs 20:17

Bread of deceit is sweet to a man; but afterwards his mouth shall be filled with gravel.

It is almost always "great fun" to get away with our sins, at least at first. When a child successfully lifts a cookie from the cookie jar against his mother's wishes, he experiences the sweet taste of stolen cookies and the joy of "getting away with it." But the consequences of his actions play themselves out over the next few hours or decades of his life. Even if his mother is a poor detective and cannot trace the crumbs to the perpetrator, the seed of deceit planted in the child's soul, unhindered, will grow into a large noxious weed that chokes his very life.

The child's mouth fills with gravel when he suffers his mother's disapproval and correction. But the lesson is far more painful for adults. For example, a man may "enjoy" an illicit affair for a season, but the disruption and destruction inflicted upon his family, his reputation, his character, and his life is simply beyond the power of words to describe. The wise will understand this principle and will not be taken by the sweet bread of deceit. Sadly, few are wise enough to make their decisions on any basis beyond the perceived, short term benefits of the contemplated action. May God help us to see through the thin veneer of deceiving temptations. It is wisdom that enables a man to taste the bitter flavor of the bread before he takes the first bite. Even our young children must learn that sweet cookies always turn into bitter, filthy mud when they are taken in deceit.

Family Discussion Questions:

1. Where might we find a man who communicates God's truth in fear and humility?

2. What happens when somebody cannot pay their mortgage, at least in America today? Why is it a risk to lend money to a stranger?

3. Give some examples of sweet bread that turns out to be gravel later on. How might we put the bread of deceit far away?

Part 162 ~ Wise Counselors and Foolish Flatterers

Proverbs 20:18

Every purpose is established by counsel: and with good advice make war.

A wise person who will accomplish good things in his life must base his decisions on wise counsel. First, he must be able to discern what are the important decisions in his life that would require these counselors. Not every decision you will make in your life is of equal importance. Choosing a spouse, buying a property, incurring debt for the first time, joining the armed forces, or choosing a form of higher education are all key decisions that will set the direction of your life. Of course, the sort of advisors you choose are important. A president or head of state must choose his advisors carefully because he will base his decisions on their counsel. He may wish to take advisors who hold to different political perspectives and come from different backgrounds. But for those who lead in the state, it is critical that they be "able men, who fear God, hate covetousness, and love the truth" (Exod. 18:21).

This calls for humility within the person asking for counsel, and it is especially hard for young people who think that they have what it takes to make the most important decisions without any input from parents or elders in their lives. Think of all the young men or young women who ignore their parents' advice and wishes in their choice of a spouse. The course they set for themselves becomes painful and destructive. That one decision brings indescribable suffering to themselves and others, the effects of which continue for decades, impacting generations after them! To understand the critical importance of our decisions and the need for counsel is basic to sound wisdom.

Proverbs 20:19

He that goes about as a talebearer reveals secrets: therefore meddle not with him that flatters with his lips.

How do you handle secrets? There are those who pick up a juicy tidbit about some other person, and they can hardly wait to share it with another. Revisiting the sinful behavior of others is generally unwise, unedifying, and even sinful. When a person gloats over the sinful failings of others, he finds it therapeutic and self-justifying for himself. But this gossip does nothing profitable for the sanctification of the saints and usually only sours relationships between brothers and sisters.

Wise and careful men will always operate on a "need to know" basis. The less said, the better. Yet the temptations are intensely strong to "spill the beans." To make a point, you might tell a story of some person's moral failure, but by giving away too many details, those listening have pretty much figured out the person's identity you pretended to hide. Or you might drop a hint or two about some piece of information you have picked up about a brother. Then, your friends proceed to pry out the remaining details of the story. You could blame your indiscretion on your friends' persistence, but your willingness to share the story was unmistakably obvious from the beginning.

Now on the flip side of gossip comes the sin of flattery. Those who are habitually unwise and less than truthful with their tongues make for unreliable and unfaithful acquaintances, and you would do well to keep a safe distance away from them. Often, slick salesmen will loosen their subjects up by flattery. They know how to make people "feel good about themselves." Then they sell them a bill of goods, either by way of their ideological teaching or by selling them material goods. Advertisements selling hair shampoo inform all the women watching that "they're worth it!" Men are encouraged to envision themselves in a shiny new sports car that brings out the suave, cool Casanova that lies within themselves. These commercial advertisements form unrealistic self-images within the minds of the buyers and in the end leave them with disappointed expectations.

Family Discussion Questions:

1. What are the most important decisions you will make in your life for which you would be foolish not to invite good counsel?

2. How much have we as a family engaged in gossip over the last month or two?

3. Have you ever been taken by advertisements that flatter?

PART 163 ~ CURSING PARENTS AND GETTING RICH QUICK
Proverbs 20:20

Whoso curses his father or his mother, his lamp shall be put out in obscure darkness.

Of those "kinder and gentler" humanists running around today, most are horrified to discover that Jesus actually affirmed the law that requires the death penalty for the son who curses his father or mother (Matt. 15:8). This is because they have predetermined their own elaborate system of morality where the honor of parents is of minor regard. Consequently, the modern humanists have destroyed marriage and the nuclear family. Their "nice" system of ethics is incapable of holding the family together, and they have their world where 70% of children are born without fathers, 70% of marriages end in divorce, and child abuse is ten times more prevalent in broken families. This is the world they construct for themselves.

But our lives are built upon God's ethics and God's perspectives of social systems. The fundamental social unit of the family cannot exist without the honor of parents, and this verse highlights the importance of this principle. How did the young Colorado killer, Matthew M., come to the point where he was so overwhelmed by darkness that he had to commit murder? He was educated at home by caring Christian parents. How could he have done this horrible act? The answer to this is simple. He turned against his parents. The man took to the Internet, publishing a public cursing of his mother and father months before he went on the killing spree. Some sins initiate a downward spiral, out of which it is almost impossible to extricate oneself. This seems to have been the case with Matthew.

Typically, youth will rebel against their parents first in their music choices. They turn to the music which their parents would find most abhorrent. This was the case for young Matthew, who preferred the demon-inspired music of Marilyn

Manson, who was himself raised by Christian parents and sent to a Christian school in his early years. When men curse their fathers and mothers, especially when they were taught biblically, God will use these men to destroy themselves and others around them. *Whoso curses his father or his mother, his lamp shall be put out in obscure darkness.* The theme of this verse is seen worked out in many public examples in the present age. When men cease to fear God, they, of course, will not fear their parents. But there is a God in the heavens, and He will not be mocked. Much of the murder, demonism, and the destruction around us is clearly linked to the gross violation of the fifth commandment. But for us, we will trust and pray both that our children will always fear the true and living God and that there will not be a single young man in our community who exemplifies the horrific rebellion described in this verse.

Proverbs 20:21

An inheritance may be gotten hastily at the beginning; but the end thereof shall not be blessed.

This proverb puts the kibosh on the get-rich-quick schemes. Any time some slick salesman tries to convince you of a get-rich-quick scheme, you should suspect the entire concept. This principle is a constant normative for us. Even in our investments, we should always prefer the tortoise to the hare, as featured in the famous fable. Of course, there are times when we must make a calculated risk with our investment capital. But if the intent is to get rich quick, and then we put all of our savings into a risky investment to accomplish that, we are clearly violating this important principle. Generally, it would be better to risk only a portion of the portfolio, while being careful with the rest of it.

Men have made millions of dollars writing books on "how to be successful in business" or "how to make a million dollars." By now, most of us have figured out that the best way to get rich quick is…to write a book on how to get rich quick! There are thousands of books on the market written in this vein. What would happen if an author tried to tell the truth? If you were to open his book on gaining material wealth, you would read one simple line, "Work really hard for a long time, and trust in God from Whom all blessings flow!" It is doubtful such a book would sell more than four or five copies.

Let us also be careful not to cater to the get-rich-quick impulse in others as we work with them in the marketplace. Otherwise, those we attract into our organizations will lack the character necessary to persevere and succeed. Hollow promises of easy wealth may create a little excitement on the front end of some marketing scheme, but it won't be long before the whole operation collapses like a house of cards.

Family Discussion Questions:

1. What is one of the foulest and most heinous violations of the fifth commandment ("Honor thy father and thy mother")? How do many young people begin to manifest rebellion against their own parents in their teen years?

2. What is an inappropriate way to gain wealth? What is the biblically appropriate path to wealth? Should we seek after wealth? Why or why not?

PART 164 ~ VENGEANCE AND MERCY BELONG TO GOD
Proverbs 20:22

Say not thou, I will recompense evil; but wait on the LORD, and He shall save thee.

As you read through the Book of Proverbs and compare the lessons contained therein with the rest of divinely revealed Scripture, you will soon discover that most of the basic truths of the entire Bible are contained in this book, in capsule form. This little book of wisdom could be called a "Pocket Bible"! The principle contained in this verse, for example, is repeated many times throughout Scripture (reference Deut. 32:35; Rom. 12:19; Heb. 10:30; Rev. 6:10).

Man is different from the animals in that he was created in God's image "in righteousness." He has a keen sense for justice, whereas dogs do not care much about injustices. Have you ever seen a dog carrying a placard calling for equal pay for dogs and cats or arguing for a political cause? Since man fell into sin, he no longer has the *right standard* for justice. He fights for the *wrong* causes, elects the *wrong* candidates to office, and argues passionately for the *wrong* positions. But he is still doing more than dogs will do. He has a commitment to righteousness and justice because he was created in the image of God.

Part of man's commitment to justice is seen in his desire to take revenge on those who have done him wrong. Let us say that a neighbor steals Joe's chickens. Now Joe is angry with the neighbor, but not because the man has violated one of God's commandments. The man has violated Joe's commandments. Therefore, Joe feels as if he must take vengeance upon this neighbor and make him pay. Joe acts out of a commitment to justice, but it is a commitment to Joe's justice and not to God's justice. If Joe were committed to God's justice, he would leave the rightful punishment (or vengeance) in the hands of God.

When people want to reserve the right to hurt somebody for hurting them, they fail to see that God is the just Judge, and they are not. They are trying to play the part of God. Suppose that one piece of dust fell on another piece of dust, breaking it in half. Does the damaged piece of dust have any right to revenge? I think we would readily see the absurdity of such an idea! Without God, we are all just random particles of matter falling through a universe of chance. If there is evil, it is because somebody has violated God's law, and if somebody has violated God's law, he must pay the God Whom he violated. Therefore, with our God-given desire for justice, let us be willing to wait upon the Lord to execute His justice in His time. Even if we are abused, tortured, or martyred for our faith, we can rest in the assurance that God will avenge every evil ever committed against us according to His timing (Luke 18:7–8). This exempts us from any inclination toward bitterness, unrest, anxiety, anger, or fear in response to the evils that men do.

But we are told in this verse to wait upon the Lord for His salvation. What does this have to do with God's avenging justice? If God will save us, He must do something about the evil that threatens to overwhelm us both spiritually and physically in this sin-laden world.

Proverbs 20:23

Divers weights are an abomination unto the LORD; and a false balance is not good.

God cares about accurate and honest weights in business transactions. What people perceive they are receiving for their goods and services should be, in fact, what they are receiving. If they believe that they are receiving one ounce of silver for twenty pounds of apples, then it should be one ounce of silver and not 0.95 ounces of silver. If somebody tricks them into believing that one piece of paper with somebody's picture stamped on it is worth more than another piece of paper with somebody else's picture stamped on it, when in truth it isn't worth any more than a piece of paper, then we have a violation of this principle. Herein lies the danger of paper money that is not backed by some known commodity of value. God wants honesty in trade, and anything short of that is a heinous, abominable crime in His eyes.

For related commentary, reference Proverbs 20:10.

Family Discussion Questions:

1. Why is it that we do not have a right to take vengeance on those who offend us?

2. What does salvation have to do with recompensing evil (verse 22)?

3. Suppose we are selling lemonade out on the road in front of our house. How might we give customers the impression they are receiving something of higher value than what they are really getting?

PART 165 ~ REVERENCING GOD'S SOVEREIGNTY AND HOLINESS
Proverbs 20:24

Man's goings are of the LORD; how can a man then understand his own way?

Some people go to the islands of Hawaii for a vacation. Some people go to work at aerospace companies. Some people go to watch a parade on July 4th. Some people go to heaven. Others go to hell. But where will you go on vacation twenty years from now? Where will you be working? Where will you go when you die? This text gives a clear and irrefutable answer to that question—"Man's goings are of the Lord." God determines your future. To anticipate all future events and to organize all of the circumstances of your life, such that you can be sure that you will be working at a certain company and vacationing in Hawaii twenty years from now, is entirely impossible. Even governments cannot assure that this country will exist in twenty years from now. So how can we plan for the future when we cannot possibly direct the future? Of course, the Christian knows that the future is in God's hands.

This does not dismiss our responsibility to plan and pray and prepare for the future. But if we forget that God is sovereign over the future, we will begin to assume that what happens in the future is either a matter of our own fallible, pitiful actions or a consequence of fate. If we cannot possibly forecast the future, and we cannot understand our own way, then what can we do? Well, certainly we can understand God's laws and apply them wisely in the situations that life presents to us. We can trust in God and acknowledge Him in all our ways. If we do this, we have confidence that God will direct our paths in the way of righteousness and life. Of course, God still directs the unbeliever, but into the paths of death and hell—because this man refuses to trust in God and acknowledge Him in all his ways. Either way, man's goings are of the Lord. The idea that God is in sovereign control of the most important aspects of life—whether we go to heaven or hell, for example—is not popular today. Nor has it ever been. But this is the clear teaching of Scripture passages like Rom. 9:10ff and John 6:44.

Proverbs 20:25

It is a snare to the man who devours that which is holy, and after vows to make inquiry.

There are some things more special to us than other things. A family picture in the hallway is more important than a pile of dog feces in the back yard, for example. Also, God's Word is holier than a cheap and sleazy novel. By the word "holy," we refer to something that is special or represents something special. It would be inappropriate to take the President's picture and use it for a dartboard, only because the picture represents a person and an office deserving of respect.

God is holier than a cow. This should go without saying, but occasionally you will still hear people take this very special adjective used for God and apply it to a cow! However, those who wish to live godly lives in a godless age must not reduce everything to the profane by a flippant use of language and by perpetual cynicism and irreverence. If we were to incorporate the expression "holy cow!" into our conversations, what does that do to the expression, "Holy God?" That man who has taken up using the term "holy cow!" may not have meant to cast disrespect upon the holiness of God. "I'm only using the term flippantly," he tells us, "I don't really mean that cows are holy." But that is precisely the point. Some words are special words, and should not be used flippantly. If every single word in our language is used in a profane and flippant way, then there are no words left that are special and holy, particularly when referring to God. "It is a snare to the man who devours that which is holy."

The Bible has a great deal to say about vows. For example, Paul takes a vow in the New Testament. Elsewhere, Solomon issues a sharp warning to those who make a vow and fail to follow through on it. God takes no pleasure in fools. It would be better not to vow than to make a vow and not fulfill it (Eccles. 5:4–5). Therefore, it is prudent not to make many vows, or what are known as "rash vows." As this text puts it, don't make a vow about something when you are unsure of what you are doing. Be sure you know what you are doing before you take on something. There is a current popular song, verging on the profane, that supplies a fine example of this sort of foolishness. In this ballad, the woman testifies to marrying a man without either her or her family even learning his name. The marriage vow especially should be taken very seriously (Mal. 2:14), and when people fail to do this, they violate the important principle contained in this nugget of wisdom.

Family Discussion Questions:

1. How do we plan for the future if we have no ultimate control over what happens in the future? Shall we neglect to plan for the future at all? What is our responsibility in relation to the future?

2. What is the overall attitude in our home? Are we cynical and irreverent? Or is there a constant sense of the fear of God that pervades our home? In what ways are we flippant in our handling of special words or sacraments?

PART 166 ~ WHAT TO DO WITH THE WICKED
Proverbs 20:26

A wise king scatters the wicked, and brings the wheel over them.

The wicked are an ever-present reality in our world. There is no sense in pretending that man is perfectible or that a utopia is possible until God re-forms a new heaven and a new earth. Therefore, it is for us to make the best of a bad situation, whether we are building families or civil governments. We must work to minimize the damage that the wicked bring to society, particularly to those societies over which we have some influence. When a wise and righteous leader takes the reins of power, he has two options:

1. He may "scatter" the wicked. When the wicked become a large enough minority that they have the wherewithal to build coalitions, they become a dangerous threat to the existing social systems. Over the last fifty years in this country, homosexuals built these coalitions to the point that now they have almost total control over the homosexual indoctrination in tens of thousands of public schools across the country. Wise public policies on the part of the civil magistrate might have discouraged homosexuals from coming to this country, and they might even have encouraged deportation. Good laws will discriminate against bad people. Of course, the converse is true as well—bad laws discriminate against good people. Now the mantra that the wicked teach the masses in our day is "celebrate diversity." So, of course, they oppose any kind of discrimination against wickedness such as homosexual acts, incestuous acts, etc. For us, however, the Bible defines that which is wicked and that which is righteous. A wise king will find ways to remove the wicked from the land. Be careful to distinguish between the duties of civil leaders and those of the rest of us. As long as these wicked men live in our cities, we have opportunity to call "all men everywhere to repentance" (Acts 17:31), being careful not to "cast pearls before swine" (Matt. 7:6).

2. But secondly, the king may also "bring the wheel over them." Clearly, the "wheel" referred to in this verse is the grinding wheel used to crush grain on the threshing floors of Israel (Is. 28:28–29). The civil magistrate is intended by God to be a "terror to evildoers" (Prov. 21:15; Rom. 13:4). In the words of Paul, the magistrate does not use the sword in vain. By the just use of the sword, dangerous men who commit capital crimes are stopped; this, of course, enables a stable, peaceful, and productive society. Nevertheless, it is not the responsibility of the magistrate to "weed out" all unbelievers (Matt. 13:28–29). But neither should he ignore all criminal behavior. In his administration of "the sword," he is mainly interested in those crimes that serve to unravel the social fabric of society and destabilize the nation.

Proverbs 20:27

The spirit of man is the candle of the LORD, searching all the inward parts of the belly.

In the spirit of every man, God has placed a shining light. The conscience acts as a searchlight shining here and there in every nook and cranny of the soul of a man. It can be suppressed. But it cannot be entirely extinguished. The first time a child lies to his parents, he will typically feel a pang of guilt. And the first time a man robs a bank or kills another person in anger, he will feel the torturous prodding of his conscience. Animals do not experience this phenomenon. But when men feel it, they respond in diverse, sometimes unusual ways. They may attempt to suppress it by more sin, by more lies to cover up the other lies. As the bank robber continues to rob more banks, he finds the cries of his conscience slowly fading away.

But there is no denying that light, so the wise man will use it to his advantage. That is, he will listen intently to the voice of his conscience. What is the voice of conscience saying concerning his own heart's motivations? On occasion, he will consider the way he reacts to criticism. Is it pride that finds the advice of others so reprehensible? He will even examine the way he listens to messages taught from the Word of God. "Why do I find this sermon boring?" he asks himself. "Why is my heart hardening to this brother as he preaches to me?" If you are open to the wise counselor of the conscience that resides within you, that conscience will illuminate the conditions of your heart and life. Wise young men and women will learn to use this valuable instrument God has placed in the heart of every person.

Family Discussion Questions:

1. What are the two things the civil magistrate can do in regards to the wicked? In light of verse 26 and passages like Exodus 22:1–4, would you consider prisons a proper use of state resources?

2. What does it feel like when conscience bothers you about a sin? What should you do when your conscience bothers you about a sin that you have committed?

PART 167 ~ GOVERNING BY MERCY AND TRUTH
Proverbs 20:28

Mercy and truth preserve the king: and his throne is upheld by mercy.

When the Old Testament refers to "the king," many think of these as prophetic references to Christ. Certainly, the Psalms are taken that way. But the Book of Proverbs is not meant to be taken as a prophetic book. It is a practical book intended to equip a young man to walk in wisdom. Whereas our Lord Jesus Christ indeed is the very wisdom of God (1 Cor. 1:26–31), we know that He does and will perfectly fulfill the wisdom communicated to us through His Word.

This text still speaks to godly leadership in the civil sphere. Governments come and go. Empires come and go. Kingdoms rise and fall. What preserves any and all attempts to organize human society is found in these two basic constituents—

mercy and truth. Truth is the basis for good law and equitable judgments. If a king would seek laws based in God's revealed truth and then insist on good witnesses and good evidence for his court cases, he would maintain a stable system of law. But as he gives up any interest in the truth, as he rejects God's laws, willfully misinterprets God's Word to His own sinful biases, and fails to adequately punish those who witness falsely in court trials, he gives up his right to rule. His kingdom will eventually collapse. Democracies are even more subject to revolution, anarchy, and collapse when the people have little or no interest in the truth. Often, the leaders are more subject to the ever-changing whims of the people than they are to truth.

But the king must also be committed to mercy. We live in an imperfect world, and should the magistrate pursue every instance of sin committed in every single household in his district, there would be nobody left to govern! Therefore, in a sinful world, a magistrate must allow for mercy. But when does he show mercy? Would it be appropriate to allow every killer and every bank robber to walk out of the courtroom scot-free to continue working their murder and mayhem in the surrounding neighborhoods and towns? On the other hand, wise elders and judges in churches and towns must never be perfectionists. What we are looking for is direction, not perfection. Always, righteous leaders will look to set their people in a good direction. Conversely, only tyrants will engage in unmerciful, revolutionary measures to bring about "a better society." This, by the way, also applies to fathers who lead their families. Should a father fail to know when to show mercy, eventually he will destroy his family. He will push his children too hard, risking rebellion, emotional breakdown, and disintegration. You may recall that this was the legacy of Rehoboam who threatened to beat his people with scorpions (1 Kings 2:11). Subsequently, he lost his kingdom.

Family Discussion Questions:

1. What are the ways in which a government official might show mercy? What would be an example of an inappropriate extension of mercy?

2. How might a father fail to show mercy in his pursuit of truth and justice?

PART 168 ~ STRENGTH, WISDOM, AND CORPORAL PUNISHMENT
Proverbs 20:29

The glory of young men is their strength: and the beauty of old men is the gray head.

After fifty to sixty years of life experiences, older men finally gain a little wisdom, but for some men this can be a bit of a let-down. For at the point when you have obtained that wisdom you need for life, now you lack the strength to get as much done. The solution to this conundrum is easy, of course. Old men need young men. This provides a huge incentive for wise mentorships (or apprenticeships). Sadly, this connection has broken down in modern society, where older men have little time to invest in younger men, and younger men have little interest in honoring older men! When the connection between generations is severed, we should certainly expect to see a sure and steady socio-economic breakdown.

More often than not, impetuous young men assume they know better and refuse the mentorships of older and wiser men. But those who take the time to sit at the feet of these wiser old men will benefit greatly, both spiritually and materially. When the energies of the young men are expended on wise projects suggested by the older men, both will profit greatly from the endeavors. This is especially true in smaller, entrepreneurial, home-based economies.

Proverbs 20:30

The blueness of a wound cleanses away evil: so do stripes the inward parts of the belly.

Such verses as these come off as unsophisticated, primitive, and even cruel to a decadent and decaying society. But we must remember that the tender mercies of the wicked, always turn out to be really cruel in the end. The Bible is realistic about the evil condition of the world around us, and we would be terribly irresponsible to simply ignore gross rebellion, drug addictions, and surly, violent thugs.

Some organizations today charge as much as $80,000 per year to care for a severely out-of-control, rebellious youth. These children become a threat to their own safety, not to mention that of their own parents and the rest of society. About all the state governments are willing to do is to drug them or imprison them if the parents throw up their hands and completely abandon the children. But some parents will resort to "authoritarian-based" programs that force the young man or woman into hard labor under trying circumstances. As a last resort, they may even apply the rod and lay down stripes upon the back of the rebel. The Bible limits corporal punishment like this to no more than forty stripes. From this verse, we learn that these stripes are cleansing. While they may not produce a truly repentant heart, they may limit the potential depths of evil to which a young man or woman could descend.

Needless to say, civil governments must be careful not to go beyond biblical limits in the jurisdiction of the family. Sometimes government agencies want to restrict families in this area of corporal punishment, but the Bible does not allow intervention until the perpetrators have violated the *lex talionis,* or the forty-stripe limit. The civil magistrate may interfere should there be instances of permanent burn scars or broken bones.

Family Discussion Questions:

1. Are there ways in which our sons might work with their fathers? What kind of commitment does our community or our church have toward older men mentoring younger men in businesses?

2. To what extent are spankings helpful in our family? Do spankings change the heart or just the external behavior of the children?

PART 169 ~ GOD RELATES TO THE HEARTS OF MEN
Proverbs 21:1

The king's heart is in the hand of the LORD, as the rivers of water: He turns it whithersoever He will.

Men who deny God's sovereignty over reality find it hard to believe that God is in control of everything all of the time. They may believe that God is in control of some things some of the time. They might even allow Him to control the flow of the rivers that flood their banks and destroy villages and farmlands. But does God have equal control over the heart meanderings of the most powerful men on earth? Impossible, they aver. Are the hearts of men outside of the control of the Creator of the universe? In this competition for sovereignty, God always wins. If God controls the flight pattern of every sparrow that falls from the sky, then of course He has control over the thought processes and policies implemented by the most powerful kings in the world. To conclude anything different is to deny the very "God-ness" of God.

But what about kings like Ahab and Herod, who worked their destructive and sinful designs? Did God for a moment relinquish control of those evil men? One thing we know about rivers is that they rarely run in a straight line. They wander here and there, eventually running their course into the sea. So it is with sinful men. At first we may view the horrible actions of powerful men with shock and confusion. But God will be sure that their evil intentions work His sovereign will. Even when they go so far as to kill the Son of God and persecute His people, our God will be sure that they do everything for the eventual good of the church. Some have said, that the blood of the martyrs becomes the seed of the church. Wherever the church has been persecuted at the hands of wicked men, it seems that God has used trials to strengthen His church.

When brothers do something evil to another brother such as selling him into slavery as Joseph's brothers did to him, God is still involved. The Scriptures tell us that "God meant it for good!" (Gen. 50:20) But we must still insist that those boys did the dirty deed out of their own "free will." That is, nobody coerced them into doing this. Nobody held a gun to their heads and forced them to do that envious and wicked thing. Yet, God was still involved. By nature, man's heart is inclined toward evil. The river of his heart will run toward evil. But our sovereign God will be sure that wherever the rivers run, the *kind of evil* that is exercised by that wicked heart will always produce good for His kingdom in the long run.

Proverbs 21:2

Every way of a man is right in his own eyes: but the LORD ponders the hearts.

Some actions are sinful and some are not. What makes an action sinful is its relationship to the law of God. Did the action conform to God's stated commandments? We cannot separate the action from the heart of the man who brought about the deed. Adulterous men have discontented, ungrateful hearts. Disobedient children are not willing to honor their parents as God's authority in their lives. What makes their disobedience sinful is their rebellious hearts, and their rebellion is in reference to God. This is why God ponders their hearts. He studies a child's heart to determine what sort of attitude that child maintains toward Him.

This becomes increasingly important as a person's actions take effect in what we call "the gray area." Some actions are easily labeled as sinful. Should a man rob a bank, it is generally clear that he broke the eighth commandment, "Thou shalt not steal." But what about the wife who refuses to order pizza in compliance to her husband's wishes because she thinks pizza is not a healthy choice? Where is her heart in this? Is she truly submitting to the laws of God, or is this just another opportunity for her to rebel against God's appointed authority in her life? The Lord ponders the hearts.

For related commentary, reference Proverbs 16:2.

Family Discussion Questions:

1. If God controls the hearts of kings, how does this conception change the way we perceive legislatures and governors that vote for things that work in opposition to liberty and righteousness? Do we fight bad bills before they are approved in the legislature? Do we try to get good leaders elected? What if bad leaders are elected? Should we be depressed about this?

2. Give several examples of how a child might obey his parents in "the gray area."

3. Children: Where is your heart in respect to God? Do you render superficial obedience or heart obedience to Him?

PART 170 ~ WHAT GOD REALLY WANTS
Proverbs 21:3

To do justice and judgment is more acceptable to the LORD than sacrifice.

This is one of the most important principles to be found in Scripture. The entire sacrificial system of the Old Testament regulated every aspect of the life of Old Testament Israel. Of course, God wanted sacrifice. Yet, He maintains a priority of expectations—and what He really wants are justice and judgment. He wants obedience to His moral laws, but he also requires just judgments from fathers, elders, and judges that lead in the land. Does He want us spending all of our time dialing in the fine-tuned elements of a worship service on Sunday morning, or does He want abortionists prosecuted in this land for the wanton shedding of innocent blood? In his inimical way, simple and straight-forward, James tells us what God really wants out of us: "Bridle your tongue. Visit the widow, and orphan in their affliction. And keep yourself unspotted from the world" (James 1:29).

Even as the Christ of the New Testament offered Himself as a sacrifice for sins, He did it in order that justice and judgment may be done. Would our Lord therefore prefer more sacrifice from us or more obedience? Rest assured that He delights in our sacrifices of praise and thanksgiving (Heb. 13:15–16), but first things first! To obey is still better than sacrifice (1 Sam. 15:22). Give Him obedience. Repent of your sins, and begin to walk in obedience. Then you should praise Him for His grace working in you both to will and to do of His good pleasure (Phil. 2:8–9)! For many of us, we spend a fair amount of time studying the Word, praying, and singing in our worship. We should ask the question, "What does our heavenly Father want of us? Is He truly pleased with all this preaching, worship, and praise?" Pastors and church teachers are especially aware of the ever-present tendency to violate this principle. Directly following an exhortation on avoiding gossip, the teacher witnesses multiple instances of contention and gossip in the body. Or after explaining at length the wonderful forgiveness of Christ, he finds people dragging their feet at forgiving their brothers and sisters in the church. Simply attending church is not what God wants. He wants us attending to the preaching of the Word *and* following through.

Proverbs 21: 4

An high look, and a proud heart, and the plowing of the wicked, is sin.

Now this is a surprising statement! Men often severely underestimate the corruption of their hearts and lives. They are in far worse shape than they think, and verses like this help to clarify the true depth of their problem. A person does not have to say a word or act in any way before he is condemned in the eyes of a holy God. Without a due regard for the Lord, and without attributing all his successes to God's grace, his every thought and action condemns him. He lives a proud life! He is characterized by pride. So he plows his fields, builds his businesses, constructs gigantic skyscrapers, and organizes powerful governments without bowing a humble knee to the Lord of the earth. He employs the brains God gave him, applying it to the raw materials God provided in the earth to hone his technology, but all the while refusing to give God the recognition for His provision. Worse yet, he uses God's resources to destroy the family and to pervert morality and justice as defined by the laws of God! So as the God of heaven looks down at man's fields, cities, and towers, He sees a whole lot of sin.

Pride is basic to man's economic systems in the modern empires. In fact, a recent survey of hiring managers in this country found the most important criteria these employers are looking for in prospective hires was not diligence, past experience, or even education. It was self-confidence. Of course, as Christians, we emphasize God-confidence over self-confidence. But the humanist empires would never be built without a tremendous confidence in man.

Much of the pride found in the economies of the wicked is rooted in education systems that are put in place for the purpose of preparing young people to build these proud economies. It takes proud schools to build proud economies. For many hundreds of years now, Western universities have refused to teach the fear of God in the chemistry laboratories. Seldom, if ever, would you find men within humanist classrooms struck with a trembling fear of God that drives them to their knees in worship and praise. These folks reject the very beginning of all wisdom and knowledge because of a deep-seated pride in their own intellectual achievements!

Family Discussion Questions:

1. How much time do we spend working to apply the Word in obedience, compared with the time we spend in personal devotions, family worship, and church gatherings? Are we giving God what He really wants?

2. How might we better apply the Word of God after a preaching and worship service? Instead of quickly forgetting everything that was said, might we lay out some applications whereby we can begin to follow through on what is being taught?

3. How does pride manifest itself in us? (Examples might include bragging, proud looks, proud thoughts, competition, sibling rivalries, etc.)

4. How might we avoid the pride that is such an essential element in modern university and seminary education?

PART 171 ~ THE ROAD TO RICHES
Proverbs 21:5

The thoughts of the diligent tend only to plenteousness; but of every one that is hasty only to want.

A man acts in terms of his character. Eventually, he will act out the content of his thoughts. So if a man begins to think slothful thoughts, over time he will live out those thoughts by a life pattern. Similarly, an adulterous man first thinks lustful, adulterous thoughts before he acts on those thoughts. Suppose a man frames his life around recreation, such that he always thinks about his weekends and his vacations. He daydreams of a time when he will never have to work again. He places pictures of tropical islands around his work area and imagines himself living the life of leisure in a lazy beach cabana. This man's thoughts will lead him to penury! Contrast that with a man whose thoughts are filled with exciting plans to plant fields, manufacture new products, minister to widows and orphans, and develop new services. This is the kind of man who cannot help but be productive and prosperous over the long haul.

The other trap that takes the slothful man is the get-rich-quick" scheme. At first, he throws himself into some task and goes at it for a month or two, or even a year or two, with the hopes of achieving success. But this man is not prepared for the hundreds of impediments he will run into as he attempts some business venture. Diligence demands persistence, and the slothful man is simply ill-equipped for this.

Proverbs 21:6

The getting of treasures by a lying tongue is a vanity tossed to and fro of them that seek death.

Everybody's life will bear some economic value to it. A man works. He buys and sells. What matters in a man's economic contributions in life is not so much what he has, or what he obtains, or what he produces. Much of the wealth of the nations today moves from hand to hand through dishonest means, and at the end of the day, not much is produced. This is particularly true when governments are involved in the deceitful maneuverings. The average "public servant" employed by the United States federal government in this country receives twice the compensation and benefits as the average employee working for private firms. Ironically, these "public servants" produce little of value for the economy. The government taxes the populace in order that these high-priced bureaucrats might regulate those who are actually producing food and other products for the rest of the economy. Not only is the government redistributing huge portions of the wealth through taxation to pay these salaries (as well as supporting millions of people on welfare), but it consumes trillions of dollars in debt. All the while, the government is promising to deliver a "strong and healthy economy." This is all a lie. An economy that runs on debt or the prospective productivity of future labor is not a wealthy economy. It is important to remember that debt-based economies produce a slave mentality and erode the character of subsequent generations. This will effectively ruin the economy.

Sometimes, human societies break down to the point where people grab whatever they can get for immediate gratification. "Eat, drink, and be merry," they say, "for tomorrow we die!" They lose the will to perpetuate their own posterity and think nothing of consuming all of the capital saved up from past generations. Their birth rates implode, as is the case in ninety developed countries around the world at present. If the purpose for life is instant gratification, why should they have children? What does the future hold for them? In the words of this wise saying, these people seek death.

Family Discussion Questions:

1. What kind of a thinker are you? What gets you excited about life? Do you look forward to work or to play?

2. Are you more interested in working hard or getting rich? What is of higher value to you?

3. If the purpose of riches for many today is instant gratification, what is the purpose for us?

PART 172 〜 THE THIEF AND THE WAYWARD MAN
Proverbs 21:7
The robbery of the wicked shall destroy them; because they refuse to do judgment.

"There is no honor among thieves," so the saying goes. No thief lives well for long because his basic ethical system is fundamentally compromised. How can you live with people who steal from each other all the time? For a while a robber may enjoy consuming the loot himself, but he will soon find that he cannot live among honest people. So he moves to a lawless neighborhood or some lawless South American

"Banana Republic" that countenances thieves like him. Wherever he goes, he will always find himself among thieves in the new place, which usually includes the tin-pot dictator or mob boss who has a penchant for abusing the community and corrupting their economy. Try as you will to oppose God's law system; you will find yourself frustrated and ruined. That's because the world is hard-wired according to God's way of life.

Proverbs 21:8

The way of man is froward and strange: but as for the pure, his work is right.

Here Solomon draws a comparison between generic "man" and the "pure man." By Adam's fall in the garden, the fundamental nature of mankind became terribly flawed, or totally depraved. It is not as if every isolated work of man is as bad as it could be. After all, helping an old lady across a street is nicer than running her down with an automobile! But short of the saving grace of God, a Boy Scout who is trained to help little old ladies across streets becomes a self-centered, arrogant man who contributes to politicians who advocate the killing of innocent children in their mothers' wombs. He might even advocate homosexual marriage, institutionalized stealing, and other abominations. As he makes his way through life, he turns this way and that way, working his way toward destruction.

The word "strange" may be better translated "guilty." Sinful man does not and cannot live without guilt. It is an inescapable part of his psyche. Therefore, many of his decisions, his policies, and his actions are directed by guilt. He tries to compensate for his guilt by more perverted and contorted ways. Even homosexual marriage, promoted by the moralistic and "well-meaning" social activists of our time, is a prime example of this. After all, isn't a committed homosexual relationship better than an "uncommitted one"? Strange and perverted indeed! Often men respond to guilt by means of sadism and masochism, both perverted attempts at atonement. Sadists are known to do cruel things to others, and masochists do cruel things to themselves. Twisting this way and that way, sinful man makes his way down the path to hell.

Yet, the pure in heart walks on the "straight and narrow." It is his willingness to honestly admit his sin and then deal with it according to God's standards that makes him pure of heart. He has nothing to hide from God or man. His heart is right with God, and that is what makes his work acceptable to God.

Family Discussion Questions:

1. Does our country countenance thievery? Is there true biblical justice for the thief here, where the Bible says that almost every thief should restitute four to five times the value of what was stolen (Exod. 22:1–4)? How important is it to live in a place that does not accommodate robbery?

2. What is the way of your life? As you look back on your life, can you see that you are conforming more and more to the commandments of God? Or are you wandering away from the paths of life?

PART 173 ~ THE NAGGING WOMAN AND WICKED FRIENDS
Proverbs 21:9

It is better to dwell in a corner of the housetop, than with a brawling woman in a wide house.

There are not many of the Proverbs that speak directly to women. The book itself is directed toward a son, although most of the book is still equally profitable for our daughters. But here is a verse that speaks to a specific sin with which many women struggle. It is the sin of discontentment that finds vent in complaining and nagging. Once the sin of discontentment has lodged itself in a woman's life, nothing can satisfy her. She always finds something to complain about, and her husband often bears the brunt of it. She complains about her father or her husband. She complains about being cooped up in the house. Then she goes to work and complains about her management and various aspects of her work. She incessantly worries out loud about her health and her financial condition. All day long, she carps on the character flaws of her children and her husband without any abhorrence toward her own wicked behavior. She slanders and gossips. She engages in judgmental hypocrisy and violations of the golden rule constantly. This woman is a living nightmare.

There is no satisfactory remedy for the poor wretch who finds himself married to this woman beyond escaping to an attic, where he must share the space with spiders and mice. This problem of the nagging woman may have contributed to the origination of the "tavern." Today, of course, men secure a bill of divorcement for "irreconcilable differences," but many years ago, divorce carried a strong stigma with it. Even today divorces can be cost-prohibitive with lawyer fees, alimony, and many other expenses. So men will do what they can to avoid their nagging wives, even to the point of spending untold hours each evening sitting on barstools "enjoying" the community of drunks.

Obviously, our sons would never want to marry one of these women, and God forbid that any of our daughters would ever grow up to be such a person! Godliness with contentment is great gain. Whether our children will live in a dirt hut or in some great mansion, they must learn to be grateful, hopeful, and content. Griping against the difficult circumstances God arranges for us is, in the ultimate sense, complaining against the wise providence of God.

Proverbs 21:10

The soul of the wicked desires evil: his neighbor finds no favor in his eyes.

If a man does not desire heaven for himself or his friends, then he must be content with the fact that they are all going to hell. When a group of college-aged young people organize a party of drunkenness and other revelries, their companionship cannot possibly involve much concern for the souls of those involved. Their friendship is empty and meaningless, for they take delight in their friends' drunkenness and debauchery, which is exactly what earns for them the damnation of their souls. Even bank robbers might enjoy a little camaraderie with their fellow thieves. But when they encourage each other in thievery, they are only encouraging their comrades in that which would ruin their lives. What applies to the temporal applies that much more to the eternal. Those who delight in the moral depravity of their friends are setting them up for failure and destruction. What kind of friend would contribute to his friend's destruction? Of course, this is no friend at all. If, therefore, a man desires what is evil for himself and his acquaintances, he will naturally have a perverted sense of friendship.

If you are a good friend, you should wish the very best for your friends—which would be nothing less than eternal life! You would never sit idly by while your friends abuse God's name or ignore His claims on their lives. You would look out for their "better interests." And as long as they are your friends, you would relentlessly pursue their better interests. Should they cast off your pleadings and grow weary of your constant witness, more often than not they will pull away from you, and you will find that friendship with unbelievers who persistently reject the truth is impossible.

Family Discussion Questions:

1. What sort of signs might we note in a four-year-old girl, a ten-year-old girl, or a fifteen-year-old girl, indicating that we might have a brawling, nagging woman in the making?

2. Contrast a godly, contented woman with the brawling woman.

3. If you are a true friend, how might you look out for the well-being of your friends?

PART 174 ~ THE IGNORANT AND THE SCORNERS
Proverbs 21:11

When the scorner is punished, the simple is made wise: and when the wise is instructed, he receives knowledge.

The debate on capital punishment rages today between the "liberal" and the "conservative." Usually, the "liberal" is the fellow who wants to be nicer than God, Who instituted the practice of capital punishment for the murderer by direct command in Genesis 9:6. But the conservative often takes the biblical stance on this without a direct appeal to the Bible. Instead, he will appropriately draw in this principle from Proverbs 21:11. It is the deterrent argument. When a murderer is hanged in the town square, others can't help but take note. It does become a powerful deterrent to the "simple" folk. Of course, there will be other rebellious scorners who will ignore all instruction. Even the sight of some murdering wretch swinging from the gallows will have little effect upon them, because *they are scorners.* But we must remember that two things are accomplished when a murderer swings. The scorner is punished and the ignorant experience an important teaching moment.

For related commentary, reference Proverbs 19:25.

Proverbs 21:12

The righteous man wisely considers the house of the wicked: but God overthrows the wicked for their wickedness.

The righteous man studies history through the eyes of a biblical worldview, always assuming that God is completely just and that He will accomplish His purposes in history. It is no secret that the wicked flourish for a while. Typically, when men gain wealth and power, they will ignore God and act in ways antithetical to God's law. Gaining power, in the minds of these men, is tantamount to displacing God. They forget that whatever power they gain is allowed them by the hand of God. But how does the righteous man view the powerful families of the wicked, whether they be a Mafia family or the Kennedy clan that ruled the United States during the latter half of the 20th century?

First, he follows Psalm 37. He knows that they will soon perish like the grass. After a hundred years or so, you will look for the legacy of the Kennedy clan, and you will not see it. What happened to Al Capone's family, descendants of the mob boss who terrorized Chicago in the 1920s? What evil are Napoleon's descendants bringing down upon Europe, two hundred years after his demise? Or what happened to Ceausescu, the evil dictator in Romania who brought so much suffering to Christians like Richard Wurmbrand in the 1950s? According to this text, the righteous man takes a long-term perspective to everything going on in the present. He remembers that "the mills of God grind slowly, but very fine." He knows that God is in control, and he muses over what He is doing in history. Of course, history is very complex, and it is doubtful that we will ever completely comprehend God's agenda. But this doesn't preclude all interpretive analysis. We know that God is the ready Judge of the earth. We also know that He is quicker to act today than in the Old Testament era. This seems to be the thrust of Paul's point in his message on Mars Hill, when he told the Athenians, "The times of this ignorance God winked at, but now He commands all men everywhere to repent" (Acts 17:30). God may have put up with the rebellion, fornication, idolatry, and ignorance of the Roman Empire for 475 years, but it is doubtful that He will put up with the modern empires for that long.

So as you consider the wealth and power of men who refuse to worship the true and living God, how will you react? Will you fear and fret? If some wicked warlord locked you away in his dungeon for twenty years, would you still be able to "wisely consider the house of the wicked"? Peering through eyes of faith, could you see the hand of God moving through history against the house of the wicked?

Family Discussion Questions:

1. Why would you punish a scorner if he will not learn his lesson in the punishment?

2. How should we view the success, power, the riches of wicked men?

3. What is the difference between God's treatment of wicked nations in the Old Testament and His treatment of wicked nations in the New Testament era?

PART 175 ~ GIVING TO THE POOR AND GIFTS FOR ANGRY MEN
Proverbs 21:13

Whoso stops his ears at the cry of the poor, he also shall cry himself, but shall not be heard.

When Jesus was here on earth, he established a pattern for all of us to follow. As the Son of God Who knew the will of His Father, He spent his days, weeks, and years helping the poor, healing the sick, and feeding the hungry. However, what is considered poor in some societies today is not what the Bible would regard as poor. For example, a person who could not afford a second automobile or dessert with every meal is not truly a poor man. The poor are those who cannot feed themselves, defend themselves, or even care for their families. A poor man is one who cannot afford to provide for himself the bare necessities of life. Or it could be somebody who is in the midst of a serious health crisis or a short-term financial crisis.

But what does a family do who receives seven pleas for help in a single day from various charitable organizations? Does this passage obligate the family to provide for each of these causes? If there were seven persons at your door crying out for help from starvation, then it would be advisable to do what you could to help them (especially if you had the resources). This passage says nothing about helping charitable organizations who have taken upon themselves the task of helping large numbers of poor people in far-flung countries around the world. Generally, the biblical idea of charity is within a local context, based in relational and accountable means.

Then there is the problem of lying beggars who refuse to live in a community where accountability is possible. The Bible assumes here an *honest* cry for help, as best as can be determined. Yet, if you are not careful you may find yourself interpreting every cry for help as fake, thereby relieving you of any obligation to help anybody. Thus, it is important that we respond to a cry for help by making honest enquiry into the matter. Do not develop the habit of ignoring cries for help. Rather, you should always be mentally prepared and willing to help somebody. One who has a heart to help others will be waiting for opportunities to assist poor people, whether they be stranded strangers on the side of the highway or widows in your own church. Occasionally, a good Samaritan gets burned by a shyster or a roadside bandit, but Jesus did promise that some would be persecuted for attempting to do good to others.

Proverbs 21:14

A gift in secret pacifies anger: and a reward in the bosom strong wrath.

Generally, most people are not inclined to help somebody who is angry. They would rather not be in the presence of an angry man because anger is usually irrational, abusive, and sometimes dangerous. Nevertheless, some families must live with the sad reality of an angry father or husband every day. This man is easily irritated. He yells and screams. He beats the walls with his fists, and he abuses with cruel words and intonations. But, remarkably, somebody leaves a little chocolate on his pillow from time to time. Somebody fixed the screen door he removed from its hinges the day before. Somebody quietly washed and ironed his clothes and left them hanging in his closet. Each time, this secret angel did the good deed without celebration, without notice, and without leaving even a trace of evidence that might indicate the source. Now, of course, the angry man seldom deserves such mercy. And it may very well have been the victim who did something good for the brute who treated her badly. But this is exactly what Jesus Christ commands. What motivates a soul to perform such things for an undeserving wretch? Of course, Jesus Christ showed us mercy even when we didn't care to seek it out. But also, remember that God is watching the entire affair. If our hearts go out to the kind, patient soul who continues to do nice things for some ungrateful, angry wretch, we know that our God in heaven is one hundred times more connected with this pitiful scene. Jesus promises a great reward in heaven for those who bear up well under persecution. We have to believe that there is something far better for us in heaven than on this miserable earth. Therefore, by a determined and resilient faith we should bear up under untoward circumstances and show mercy even to those who themselves are not likely to show mercy.

But this text promises that these sorts of deeds will make some progress toward pacifying the anger. It might not rid the home entirely of these outbursts. But if there was anything that would quell the tirades, this would do it. Of course, it is extremely rare to find a righteous person with the wisdom and the grace to respond to anger in this manner. Most of the time, anger just spawns more anger. Sometimes, a wife will try to rebuke her husband when he "loses it." She may try to reason with him. Almost always these responses are futile and even counter-productive. If his anger verges on the violent, she may do well to remove herself and her children from the area. Beyond this, the wisdom presented in this verse will be the most effective response to anger.

Family Discussion Questions:

1. Are we obligated to give money to every charitable cause in the country? What is our obligation to help the poor? Does our family show enough compassion to the poor in our neighborhood or church?

2. How might you judge an "honest" cry for help?

3. How does Jesus look upon someone who tries to help somebody else only to find out that he has been used by a shyster?

4. When somebody raises his voice around you and speaks in anger, how might you be tempted to respond? What is the better way to respond?

PART 176 ~ GOD'S JUDGMENT
Proverbs 21:15

It is joy to the just to do judgment: but destruction shall be to the workers of iniquity.

Three things mark the life of the righteous man—doing justly, loving mercy, and walking humbly before God (Mic. 2:8). The just man delights greatly in the commandments of God. But they are more than hypothetical for him. He loves to see these laws worked out in concrete reality. He wants to *do* what is just and right in every aspect of his life—in his marriage, his business life, and his civic life. Should he hear about a bloody murderer who is ravaging and murdering young women in his neighborhood or even in his house, he does not sit idly by and let it happen. He cannot ignore such a thing. Before God, he has an obligation to preserve the lives of others and to see that justice is done in this situation. But what is the righteous way? What is a just judgment is such a case? Biblical passages such as Exodus 22:2 and Deuteronomy 19:11–13 and 22:25 are helpful to determine the course of justice. There ought to be a measure of joy when a righteous judge draws a just verdict based upon good evidence and solid witnesses. Even the executioner who pulls the lever to end the life of a murderer should do so with confidence and joy, knowing that he is executing the righteous laws of God. Destruction shall be to the workers of iniquity.

Proverbs 21:16

The man that wanders out of the way of understanding shall remain in the congregation of the dead.

There is not much data to be found in the Old Testament concerning the final state, but this verse gives just a sliver of a picture for us. Evidently, there is a place known as the "congregation of the dead," and some will remain there forever. Our Lord spoke of a place where the worm never dies and the fire is never quenched; a place where there will be weeping and gnashing of teeth, and a place of unimaginable agony and hopeless, eternal death. And according to this verse, the inhabitants of such a place will include those who "wander out of the way of understanding."

Apparently, there are some who have access to the way of understanding before they wander away from it. These would include any child who had access to the teaching of the Word of God. This can happen in various ways. For example, a young man may decide one morning to pack up his things, run away from home, and never return to his Christian home or to any church at all. Or he may, over a long period of time, fade away from the way of truth. During his later teen years, he may sit in the back row of the church and check out the girls. During his college years, he makes it to church once a month or so. Later in his twenties, he attends a trendy, post-modern church that refuses to call men and women to repentance in regard to the relevant sins of the day. Finally, as he reaches his later fifties, he is nowhere near the highway of understanding. Despite the fact that several relatives reach out to him with "the Gospel," he will have nothing to do with it. This story has been repeated millions of times over the last generation or two in this country during the Great Apostasy in the West (1900s–2000s).

Family Discussion Questions:

1. What is a righteous judgment for a murderer, as defined by the laws of God?

2. How does the righteous man feel when he has opportunity to pursue the just judgments of God?

3. How do you feel when you know you have done the right thing, that which God has commanded?

4. How might a young man raised in a Christian home wander from the way of understanding? (Without giving names, you might relate typical stories of apostasy that have occurred in your experience.)

PART 177 ~ AN INFATUATION WITH PLEASURE
Proverbs 21:17

He that loves pleasure shall be a poor man: he that loves wine and oil shall not be rich.

All of us enjoy some of the pleasures of life, whether they be food, drink, or entertainment. But some become addicted to pleasure. The comforting feeling of food passing down into the digestive system or the pleasure of visual stimulus from the movie screen can be addictive. Even fiction novels (whether they are fantasy or science fiction) can be as addictive as alcohol. For many, these pleasures serve as an escape from reality. But more often people will become addicted to the "good feeling." They don't understand that merely stimulating the right nerve endings will never provide them with a deep and long-lasting sense of fulfillment. So they just keep seeking satisfaction from these superficial sources of pleasure.

When a man's chief end in life becomes the superficial pleasures of food and drink, he will seek them with all his heart and with all his strength. The problem, of course, is that these pleasures will cost him something, for nobody will ever enjoy the fruits of the earth without first cultivating the earth. Therefore, as a man fixates upon the fruits of labor without focusing equal energies at producing those fruits, he will be reduced to poverty.

Proverbs 21:18

The wicked shall be a ransom for the righteous, and the transgressor for the upright.

A ransom is a payment by which a person is released from the bondage of slavery. We know that we are released from the slavery of sin by means of the ransom payment of Christ. But what does it mean for the wicked to serve as a ransom? It is important to remember that God's judgment is both individual and corporate. Sometimes, God targets entire groups of people that are in revolt against Him. For example, the rise of homosexuality in the latter part of the 20th century in the decadent Western nations saw a concomitant increase in the incidence of the AIDS disease. Over a period of thirty years, this disease killed at least 600,000 people in this country alone. With very few exceptions, the disease was confined to homosexuals and the promiscuous. Thus, those who remained pure of this destructive behavior were protected from the judgment of God.

Occasionally, God does bring judgment upon both wicked and righteous at the same time, as in the case of the

Babylonian exile, where men like Daniel, Shadrach, Meshach, and Abednego were all uprooted and transported to a foreign, hostile land. Other times, however, the wicked will take the brunt of the judgment. This is apparently the case with the homosexual problem in Western nations. One way or another, God must deal with wicked communities, and sometimes the wicked become a ransom for the righteous.

Family Discussion Questions:

1. How do we handle pleasure? Is there a tendency among us to be fixated upon things like food or entertainment? What are our chief desires in life?

2. What does it mean for the wicked to serve as a ransom for the righteous? In general, does righteous behavior lead to longer lives? (Reference the fifth commandment.)

PART 178 ∽ A CURSED HOUSE AND A BLESSED HOUSE
Proverbs 21:19

It is better to dwell in the wilderness, than with a contentious and an angry woman.

There is a slight difference between these words and those contained in verse 9 above. This woman is angry. Discontentment and contention is one thing, but add anger to that and you have a real problem on your hands. An angry man or an angry woman leave the same scourge to any home. Anger, however, will take on different forms in men and women. For a woman, anger plays itself out through cutting, wounding words or by trying to manipulate emotions in those around her. If this kind of behavior continues unchecked, it will result in disastrous effects on relationships and families.

Often, a young girl who suffered a bad relationship with her own father will become an angry, bitter woman in her adult years. She may have been scorned by her father, or she never felt any true love and affection from him. He may have been insensitive and rude, even slamming the door in her face. Of course, none of these circumstances would excuse the sin of her anger, but they may have created an environment in which great colonies of anger bacteria could multiply.

The first step to solving the anger problem is to confess the sin and the horrible effects of it to those whom you have offended. Identify all the roots of it, including all those thoughts and sentiments that disturb the peace and create turmoil in your heart. Ask yourself, "Why do I get so upset about everything? Why can't I accept the inconveniences and trials God brings to me with contentment, peace, and joy?" Where is your hope for eternal life? Where is your faith? Why do you want to control everything and everybody around you? Can't you be satisfied with everything being under God's control?

For related commentary, reference Proverbs 21:9.

Proverbs 21:20

There is treasure to be desired and oil in the dwelling of the wise; but a foolish man spends it up.

Several verses earlier, we were warned not to "love" oil. At the time these wise sayings were first recorded, such possessions were considered luxuries, as it would take a fair amount of work to extract medicinal or cosmetic oils out of plants. How does this then comport with the instruction not to "love oil"? Today our materialistic culture is still as infatuated with cosmetic cologne as they were 4,000 years ago. It is only that we have better packaging today, along with four-foot glamour photographs of sensuous women advertising the perfumes. But you see, these advertisements are geared for those whose hearts are drawn to these things for their own pleasure. Still, there is nothing essentially sinful or evil about perfumes and colognes, gold and silver, houses and cars, or anything else that is either useful or valued by humans. The difference between the wise man and the foolish man is just this: the foolish man is a consumer. He consumes everything he earns because he is a pleasure addict. He would have a hard time agreeing with the Apostle Paul, "Having food and clothing, therewith to be content." Conversely, the wise man conserves what he has and doesn't need to use it all up on himself. He saves for a rainy day. He waits until he finds somebody truly in need, and he uses his goods to help them in the best way he can. Herein is some of the wisest financial advice you will ever find. Our children must learn self-control in finances and good wisdom in saving their investments. Material riches and investments are only gifts to be employed in the service of Christ to the glory of God. We hold them in one position only until we find a better place where they might be employed for the good of the kingdom of God! Often we do use our goods to take care of our bodies, feed our families, and put a roof over our heads. But even this must be for the good of the kingdom of God and its righteousness (Matt. 6:33). We may hold it in the form of gold or silver for awhile, but eventually we will transfer the value into a business that builds homes or manufactures products. Or we will give it to our children to build households for the kingdom, or we may pass it along to ministries that are engaged in the worthwhile project of discipling the nations (Matt. 28:18–20).

While there are the consumers who worship at the feet of the material-god, don't forget that there are also those who worship the things they treasure up in their homes and savings accounts. Either way, we are dealing with the sin of idolatry. Spend thrifts and misers are both idolaters. A balanced sense of materials will only come when our chief delight and the object of our worship and service is God Himself.

Family Discussion Questions:

1. What are the various ways a woman might express anger?

2. How might you deal with the problem of anger in your life?

3. Why is it important to save some wealth in your home? At what point can you say that you are being stingy with your things? How do we avoid idolatry in relation to our material things?

PART 179 ~ SEEKING GOD'S KINGDOM AND HIS RIGHTEOUSNESS
Proverbs 21:21

He that follows after righteousness and mercy finds life, righteousness, and honor.

This short statement of doctrine beautifully summarizes the way of salvation for the true believer. He is the seeker of righteousness and mercy. With all his heart, he seeks after these two things! He wants to be considered righteous, to be righteous, and to do righteousness. But he knows that without mercy, there is no way a sinner will ever achieve any of this righteousness.

Jesus told us to seek, and we would find. Applying this to the present subject, if you will not seek after righteousness and mercy, you most certainly will not find them—nor will you find life, righteousness, and honor. Thus you can see the problem with the average person. He seeks after the wrong things. Instead of seeking after mercy, he looks for more self-esteem and self-aggrandizement. Rather than seeking after righteousness, he seeks his own happiness and material well-being in the sort of things after which the Gentiles seek (Matt. 6:30–33).

Proverbs 21:22

A wise man scales the city of the mighty, and casts down the strength of the confidence thereof.

Man builds his great cities by pride. Something has to motivate men to do outstanding feats, and pride or honor is key in this. When Ernest Shackleton set out upon his exceedingly dangerous mission to Antarctica, he promised fame for his men in case of success. The great playwright William Shakespeare immortalized the words upon which empires are built when his *Henry V* refused to share the honor with yet one more man from England! "If it is a sin to covet honor, I am the most offending soul alive," he cries.

So you can see that it is pride, honor, and material success that will spur men on to incredible feats requiring reservoirs of courage, daring, and superhuman effort. This is what it takes for humanist man to build his institutions, governments, and economies.

What then do Christians have to do with these great powers? Do wise men have a place here, where pride and lust dominate just about every institution? Yes. According to this text, their role is to cast down the strength of the confidence thereof. Where proud men break God's laws with impunity, a wise man must figure out how to cast these things down. If a wise man casts down the strength of the confidence of these cities, to what end does he do this? Of course, this wise man isn't a destructive anarchist at all. Rather, he is bringing down the pride. He works hard to decentralize the power systems, stripping back the power of tyrants whose solutions are always found in centralizing power. Human pride always leads to autonomy and a rejection of God's laws. So the wise man sets out to establish humble institutions, governments, and industries. He would prefer family economies to large corporate, institutionalized systems. He advocates one-on-one discipleship over large, proud universities, whose goal is to mass-produce proud and smart technicians for constructing large, centralized systems. Therefore, this man will institute mentorship programs within corporations, for example. He will disciple college students within the universities. If he is elected to serve in powerful civil governments, he serves with humility and works to reduce his power and decrease his budgets, thereby pushing power downhill. These are not easy tasks, but the wise man will find a way to bring it about.

Family Discussion Questions:

1. What things do we seek after more than anything else in life? What does the Bible promise to those who will seek?

2. What is the chief motivating factor in the lives of those humanists who build large empires? How does the Christian differ from the humanist?

PART 180 ~ BRIDLING THE TONGUE AND PROUD WRATH
Proverbs 21:23

Whoso keeps his mouth and his tongue keeps his soul from troubles.

The source of most of the world's problems comes from the tongue. How many disastrous circumstances could have been avoided had it not been for somebody's flapping jaws? Broken relationships, wars, failed missionary efforts, divorces, and fragmented church ministries are almost always consequences of the improper use of the tongue. How much devastation could be avoided if people would just learn the lesson of bridling the tongue! Indeed, the unbridled tongue is a world of iniquity, a fire from hell that burns and burns, destroying everything in it path (James 3:6). Relationships that took twenty years to build can be burned to the ground in one day!

In this business of guarding the lips, four sentinels are commissioned, and each must ask a different question. "Is what I am about to say really true? Is it loving? Is it necessary? And is it wise?" If all four of these sentinels are not satisfied, then it would be wise not to say anything at all. If you are responding out of anger or fear instead of love, then hold your peace. Just stop talking. Do not say a word until you know that you speak out of love. If you do not know the right thing to say, do not say anything at all. The sentinel in charge of the question, "Is it necessary?" needs to hold that tongue! Although the silence may seem a little awkward at first, you should not feel compelled to say something to fill the "dead air." Learn to be comfortable with a moment of silence or a moment to reflect. Speak only when you have something helpful or something edifying to say. These are all hard lessons to learn, probably harder than learning your multiplication tables in school. But these lessons are far more important than anything you ever learned in a mathematics class.

Proverbs 21:24

Proud and haughty scorner is his name, who deals in proud wrath.

Typically, pride combined with wrath produces a fairly dangerous individual. Pride seeks power, but wrath uses that power to destructive ends. Perhaps the best example of this in biblical history is the tyrant Haman, found in the book of Esther. His pride is legendary, but his anger against Mordecai and the Jews was unquenchable. Once he had the king's favor and a position of power, he would stop at nothing less than annihilation of the Jews. Once a man is overwhelmed by pride and impelled by wrath, he will stop at no warning, rebuke, prophetic pronouncement, or legal restraint, as he pursues his destructive agenda. Whether it be a mad dictator in Zimbabwe or an enraged postal clerk firing off an AK-47 rifle at his coworkers in Peoria, Illinois, there comes a point at which the only thing that will stop this scorner is a bullet through the head (or a hanging from the gallows). Wrath is one thing, but proud wrath is impossible to curb or correct, and it is dangerous.

As parents, it is essential that we correct the first signs of anger in our children. But we should also look for a willingness to *be corrected!* Should wrath be combined with an unwillingness to receive correction, we have a dangerous scorner on our hands. In such cases, parents may be pressed to turn their son over to the civil magistrate (Deut. 21:18–21).

Family Discussion Questions:

1. How much time do we spend working on bridling the tongue? What are the four sentinels? Have you trained these guardsmen to put a guard on your tongue?

2. Give several examples of proud, wrathful men in biblical history. Why is the proud, wrathful man so dangerous?

PART 181 ~ THE ROOT OF SLOTHFULNESS
Proverbs 21:25

The desire of the slothful kills him; for his hands refuse to labor.

Already, the Book of Proverbs has covered many lessons on the matter of slothfulness and diligence. Physical and spiritual slothfulness are fundamental sins. But now, we get to the root of the problem with the slothful man. He desires "not to work." It's just that simple. He doesn't want to work. Every day he sits and longs for vacation. He wants to play his games and enjoy his entertainments.

The Apostle points to the sin of idleness as a reason for excommunication or "dis-fellowshipping" from the body of the church (2 Thess. 3:6ff). "If any will not work, neither shall he eat," says Paul. Of course, there are blind and lame men who cannot work. But the slothful man has no desire to work, as proven by his refusal to perform menial tasks offered him. Although he may already be poverty stricken, this man may not be invited to the church fellowship meals, and certainly the church ought to exclude him from its charitable offerings. Naturally, it is a sad thing to watch a slothful man starve himself to death. But remember, it is the desire of his heart that kills him. As we watch him die of starvation, we cannot help but think, "What a cruel and wicked heart that should kill a man like that!"

Hence, as parents deal with slothfulness in the home, they should pay close attention to the hearts of their children. Where are their hearts' desires? Are they more drawn to their play than to their chores? Slothfulness is a terrible sin, but Jesus came to save us from sins like this. When the Lord Jesus saves our children from sins as bad as this one, He saves them from the sin that would kill them!

Proverbs 21:26

He covets greedily all the day long: but the righteous gives and spares not.

Ironically, the slothful man is also a covetous man and a hoarder. His hollow, hungry eyes and greedy hands grasp whatever little bit of material goods he has scraped together in his life. Fearing that he will lose whatever he has, he cannot possibly bring himself to share with others. The blessed life of prosperity and generosity that God has designed for men all comes apart with the slothful man. As sins begin to compound in the life of this man, he becomes a miserable, frustrated, tight-fisted little wretch. Should he fail to repent of these sins, he will die a miserable man.

But the economic life of the righteous man is far different from what has been described in the last several proverbs. His goal is to work with his hands so that he might have means to give to him that has nothing (Eph. 4:28). His life is "others-focused." Life is work, but it is more than that. He works to make money, yes, but it is not to deck his home with expensive furnishings or his coffin with fine silk. What motivates him to get out bed on Monday morning is that he might make somebody else's life more blessed. It is to help the helpless, the widow and the orphan. So you can see the root problem with the slothful man is that he is self-consumed, and he sees the widow and orphan hardly reasons to motivate him to get out of bed and start producing something!

Family Discussion Questions:

1. What is the root issue with the slothful man? What must we do when we begin to see this root issue in our own hearts?

2. Why is the slothful man also a covetous man?

3. Why do we go to work?

Part 182 ~ False Sacrifices and False Witnesses
Proverbs 21:27

The sacrifice of the wicked is abomination: how much more, when he brings it with a wicked mind?

Our lives are made up of two things: life and worship. Although we do glorify God in the mundane aspects of life as in eating and drinking, it is still appropriate to distinguish between life and worship. There are times at which we bring a sacrifice to God in an act of worship. In the Old Testament era, these sacrifices were typically burned or presented to God at the temple in Jerusalem. But today, we carefully prepare sacrifices of thanksgiving and praise (Heb. 13:15–16; Eph. 5:19–20), which we offer to Him in the context of the church (2 Cor. 9; Gal. 6:10). What can we say about churches that support homosexuality—churches filled with homosexuals singing "Amazing Grace"—and at the same time support orphanages? This strange phenomenon marks certain segments of the apostate church today. From their advertisements, we find that these "homosexual churches" subscribe to the Trinitarian doctrines, the two natures of Christ, and salvation by grace and through faith. Of course, these abominable assemblies will die out as quickly as the curse of homosexuality dies. Within twenty or thirty years, these social systems will disintegrate, and anybody reading this account two hundred years from now will scarcely believe that these "churches" ever existed.

So these wicked men and women sing the *Doxology* or the *Gloria Patri* in their assemblies. Their sacrifices are received by heaven as one would receive a gift of dog feces. Every dollar they place in the offering to support the orphanage fund is just one more stinking excretion. Of course, the root problem is the same heart issue reflected in King Saul when he brought his sacrifice to God. His generosity was laced with his own autonomous rebellion. At heart he did not want to humbly submit to God and repent of his sins. Several years ago, one of the leaders of these homosexual churches was protesting outside of a large Christian family ministry in Colorado Springs. The local press reported on his angry protest against the ministry's position against the sin of homosexuality. The homosexual "pastor" told the press, "These people think there is something terribly wrong with us that needs to be fixed." Although this man considered such a notion utterly despicable, for us this is a true summary of the Gospel of Christ. There is something terribly wrong with all of us, that needs to be fixed. These people just refuse to humble themselves and admit the utter bankruptcy of their condition. In their pride, they could not possibly admit that their social systems were so fundamentally flawed that they have sunk to the level of committing the ultimate social abomination (Gen. 18:20, 19:5; Judges 19:22; Lev. 18:22, 27, 20:13). The sin of homosexuality is bad enough, but the pride that refuses to face the horrid nature of one's own sin is far worse!

Yet, how is the homosexual church different from the church that refuses to confront the sin of disrespectful children? Or what about the church filled with bitterness and gossip, where elders are themselves so wrapped up in it that they wouldn't dare preach against it?

Proverbs 21:28

A false witness shall perish: but the man that hears speaks constantly.

The Hebrew word used for our English word "hear," denotes a careful, attentive listening that is intent to know the real facts of the case. This is in contrast with the false witness who doesn't really care about the truth. He listens haphazardly and never really ascertains the truth himself. According to Romans 10, faith comes by hearing, and hearing comes by the Word of God. So to be a good witness of the truth, you must first receive the truth by hearing the truth. You must carefully listen to the truth so you can get your facts straight. There are plenty of false witnesses who grab a few ideas from the Bible and construct their own little cults and sects. At the end of the day, you discover that they were not interested in framing their understanding of truth and reality by the revelation of God. From the outset, they may have borrowed a few neat biblical terms that made them sound "spiritual," but their intent was to come up with their own version of the "truth." Even though these sects may have collected a following of 250,000 people, their efforts are all vain in the end, and they join the ranks of the thousands and thousands of religious sects that have led millions down another path to hell.

Now, what about us? We must begin with a careful attentiveness to the Word of God. It is not for us to grab a few isolated texts and create our own religion out of them. Our true desire is to humbly listen to the instruction of the Spirit of God through the reading of the Word. Continually, our minds are open to the correction and instruction of the Word (2 Tim. 3:16–17). We will be perpetually transformed by the renewing of our wills, that we may prove what is that good, and acceptable, and perfect will of God (Rom. 12:2). Then we can speak. And when we speak, our words will carry a force that will transform the lives of others for eternity.

Family Discussion Questions:

1. Are we really confronting our own sin in our churches? Does God receive our worship as from sincere, humble hearts of repentance?

2. How does true faith come (according to Romans 10)? What is the basic problem with the heretic who wants to start up his own little cult?

3. How careful are we to really listen to the Word of God?

Part 183 ~ Opposing God vs. Trusting God and Walking in His Way

Proverbs 21:29

A wicked man hardens his face: but as for the upright, he directs his way.

The Bible distinguishes just two groups of people in the world, both in the Old and New Testaments. There is no middle ground here. Either you are a sheep or a goat, wheat or a weed, a wicked man or an upright man. As you read through these passages, you will hear the questions again and again, "Who are you? Which side are you on?" The Word contrasts the wicked and the upright using a hundred different categorizations. Here, for example, the wicked man hardens his face and refuses to humble himself before God. Whenever you sin, you may respond to guilt in one of two ways. You can either humble yourself and repent before God, Whose law you broke, or you can harden your heart and steel yourself in your disobedience. The wicked man chooses the latter approach. Each time he breaks the commandment, he further commits himself to his rebellion.

Just as a man walking through a minefield checks each step oh so carefully, the upright man is careful and conscientious with each step he takes. If he takes a wrong step and finds himself on an explosive mine, he will not commit to taking that step with the entire weight of his body. The wise man backs away, repents of his waywardness, and takes a different direction through the minefield of life. Thus, the difference between the upright and the wicked is obvious. The wicked man takes a wrong step and commits himself to it. Not so with the righteous.

Proverbs 21:30

There is no wisdom nor understanding nor counsel against the LORD.

This text plainly says it is impossible to take up counsel against Yahweh. But how can this be when Psalm 2 speaks of the "kings of the earth taking counsel against the Lord and His Anointed"? Of course, men will attempt to thwart God and the purposes of His kingdom. They killed His Anointed One, but that was only to bring about the blood redemption of His people, according to the predetermined counsel of God! They persecute His saints, but that is only to grow His church. Wherever the powers of men attempt to persecute saints, they only serve to further strengthen the church of Christ. Whether they like it or not, the kings of the earth are working well within the counsels of God even as they take counsel against the Lord and His Anointed!

Who in their right mind would ever want to oppose this God if they knew that their opposition would only serve to advance His cause? Actually, you have two alternatives. Oppose God and advance His cause before He destroys you, or trust Him, love Him, walk with Him, and keep His commandments. Which of these makes for a sensible way of life?

Proverbs 21:31

The horse is prepared against the day of battle: but safety is of the LORD.

How much more does this exhortation apply today than it did three thousand years ago! Ancient armies consisted of men on horses, and these provided formidable defenses and offenses for the nations. But one modern bomber could wipe out ten thousand horses inside of a few minutes. Psychologically, among those who populate the larger nation-states, there is far more trust in governments and princes today than ever before. The hearts of men prostrate themselves before governments far sooner than they would cry out to the God of the heavens for His protection. After all is said and done, the strength of the nations is almost never attributed to the sovereign hand of God (at least if you read the university history books, listen to news broadcasts, or tune into the legislative committee hearings at the Capitol). The people's trust is set upon their own towers, firepower, and fleets. But no matter how well-prepared a nation may be against attacks, internal or external, it is impossible to plan for every contingency.

There is a sense of security that automatically comes with the sheer size of armies and nations, but history cautions us not to get comfortable. The great Ottoman Empire fell to a handful of men at the Battle of Malta. Famously, Napoleon met his end at Waterloo. Then, a few terrorists almost brought the American empire to its knees with the coordinated attacks on the World Trade Center in 2001, precipitating a buckling of the economy. Our lesson is as relevant today as it was with some small city-state in the days of Abraham. Trust in the Lord over every other source of strength.

Family Discussion Questions:

1. What happens when you are convicted of a sin? What is your reaction? Do you harden your heart in your sin? Do you come up with excuses and continue committing the sin? Or do you carefully contemplate your steps?

2. When wicked men set out to oppose God, what does He do with their puny efforts to oppose His agenda?

3. Read an article from the newspaper concerning national relations or present day wars. Read a history lesson from some textbook on the Civil War or some other great war. Is there any recognition of God's sovereign hand over the armies of the nations? What causes one nation to overcome other nations? Is it the manufacturing base? Is it access to nuclear bombs and other weapons of mass destruction? Or is it the sovereign hand of Almighty God?

PART 184 ~ TRADING WEALTH FOR RELATIONSHIPS
Proverbs 22:1

A good name is rather to be chosen than great riches, and loving favor rather than silver and gold.

This is a proverb that speaks with tremendous force to those living in highly prosperous, materialistic nations today. These are the nations that have systematically dismantled the family over the last six generations. They have destroyed family economies, family farms, and inter-generational connections. They have created a world where 64% of children under six are "latchkey"—which means that both father and mother are working full-time jobs and are unavailable to their children during the daytime hours. Thanks to the breakdown of marriages and family relationships, 70% of children are not raised by both fathers and mothers in this country. At one time, war and poverty turned small percentages of children into orphans. But today it is the curse of wealth that destroys these family relationships. Also, the breakdown of family relationships has produced a breakdown in the faith, with 80–90% of children from Christian homes abandoning the church as they leave home (according to recent surveys).

Material wealth trumps family relationships in far too many instances. For a time it looked as if we could sacrifice human relationships for big houses and big corporate systems that would build a high-tech world and buttress strong economies. But in the end we discovered that without strong family relationships, the character of the nation would suffer greatly. And as the character of the nation disintegrates, our debt-laden, high-tech society will eventually collapse—proving once again the wisdom of this Word.

In a biblical hierarchy of ethical values, two things are more important than materials: reputation and relationships. If you ever get an opportunity to trade wealth for your reputation or exchange economic gain for a moral principle, you ought to take it. If you are able to sacrifice material gain for family relationships or opportunities to mentor your son in business and disciple your children properly, you ought to take it. This is not to say that you should starve your family to death in the process, for part of the goal of maintaining good relationships would include keeping your family alive!

Sometimes families will sacrifice relationships on the altar of materials by giving in to ungodly anger when belongings are broken or misplaced. Should a little boy run his bicycle into his father's new $32,000 boat, he might bear the brunt of his father's wrath. We quickly discover that the father is more interested in the boat than in a relationship with his son—and his son's relationship with God. The root problem is idolatry, for the man's heart is wrapped around that boat, such that he would say cruel and hurtful things to his son who did not honor and serve the boat with the kind of devotion he wished.

Family Discussion Questions:

1. Describe a man who prefers riches to a good reputation.

2. Have our relationships been hurt by excessively busy schedules or an inordinate pursuit of wealth?

3. How do we handle our relationships when others break our things or misplace them?

Part 185 ~ A Biblical View of Social Classes
Proverbs 22:2
The rich and poor meet together: the LORD is the maker of them all.

People tend to make a big deal out of social classes. The communist philosopher Karl Marx looked at all of human history in terms of class warfare, and the Indian caste system is built entirely on a system of social classes. But Christians have a different way of looking at human society. Social class and wealth status are mere incidentals when considered from the viewpoint of the Creator. In the words of Job, "Naked came I out of my mother's womb, and naked I return thither" (Job 1:21). For that very short duration of time between birth and death, a man may collect a few marbles and a few bricks of gold, but what really matters is his standing before God on that last day. Both rich and poor will meet together at the final judgment, and what good will riches do them at that time? What will it profit a man if he gains the whole world and loses his own soul?

Difficult though it may be for those who are accustomed to interacting with people in terms of class, Christians must learn to ignore these categories when they come together in Christ. They worship the same God. They serve one another with their assorted resources and spiritual gifts. They have all received of the same unspeakable Gift, the infinite worth of divine forgiveness by the blood of Jesus. If we have a right to call ourselves the body of Christ and a true church, there must not be any strain of envy giving birth to strife among us. If there is a reticence to give up all for Christ (including our energies, money, time, and other gifts), then we must simply remind one another again that Jesus gave up all for us. Each one is needed in the body, and everyone plays an important part. If all were rich, there would be little humility. If all were poor, there would be far less charity.

The goal of biblical economics is not the elimination of wage discrepancies. Christians are not egalitarians or equalitarians. You see, poverty reminds us of our need for God. Whether we must bear the burden of our own poverty or bear the burdens of others who are struggling economically in the church, we are continually reminded of our need for God's help. We cannot solve the problem of poverty unless we solve the problem of sin. Therefore Jesus says, "The poor you will always have with you." Since humanist man set out to create his socialist utopias in the 1800s, he has attempted to eliminate the need for reliance upon God. In this country, Franklin D. Roosevelt's New Deal and Lyndon B. Johnson's Great Society programs set out to eliminate poverty. Now, years later, it's obvious that they have only made things worse. In 1960, only 6% of children were born without fathers. Fifty years later—after all of these government programs worked their sinister ends—41% of children are born without fathers, and more people are sunk into the abyss of poverty.

Family Discussion Questions:

1. Should Christians set a goal to eliminate poverty from their churches and communities? What should be the ultimate goal of Christian ministries? Do the government programs geared to eradicate poverty really achieve that end?

2. Are there rich and poor people meeting in your church gatherings? How would you describe a rich person or a poor person in your social setting? Is there relative peace and mutual edification between these classes, or do we deal with problems of envy?

PART 186 ⁓ WHAT THE FUTURE HOLDS FOR US
Proverbs 22:3

A prudent man foresees the evil, and hides himself: but the simple pass on and are punished.

It would be nice to have the gift of prophecy, to know for sure what would happen in the future. Since we are not God—the only One Who has a complete grasp on the future—this kind of infallible knowledge regarding future events is limited to that which we find in inspired Scripture. Nevertheless, we are still interested in what happens in the future. We could not act today if we didn't think our actions had some impact on tomorrow and the day after tomorrow. We plant seed, predicting that we will harvest a crop in a few months. We invest our money, hoping that it will yield us some interest. Predicting the future is a vital part of life.

Good and careful discernment are rewarded in order to make wise predictions. This discernment is based on something more than experience; it must be rooted in God's Word. We see the dark clouds gathering, so we forecast a storm. But is it possible to see the dark clouds gathering as immoral people take over our institutions? As relationships sour in a church, the wise man will discern an ungodly spirit of dissension that could rip the church to shreds. Knowing that God's patience rightfully wears thin with nations in apostasy, we might come to the conclusion that our own nation is at risk of severe judgment. For generations now, American Christians have expected some judgment upon our nation which has forgotten God. How can a nation kill its children and institutionalize sodomy as a preferred lifestyle while expecting to escape the judgment that fell upon a child-sacrificing, Baal-worshiping Israel or a decadent Sodom thousands of years ago? If God "winked" at some of the sins of the Old Testament era, but now He commands every man everywhere to repent (Acts 17:30), then nations would do well to repent—immediately. Yet, repentance is hardly talked about, even among church-going people. This does not bode well for the future of a nation that has run headlong into sins that are particularly egregious to God.

In a day where weapons of mass destruction are in the hands of sinful men, the prudent will do well to not place absolute trust in princes or in the United Nations. The nature of sinful man hasn't changed since the garden, and now he has access to powerful weapons that could destroy entire cities. Of course, this does not mean that we should live in fear of men. Not at all! We take careful note of our circumstances and do our best to protect our own families in days of trouble. We will "trust in God and keep our powder dry," as Oliver Cromwell once said.

Proverbs 22:4

By humility and the fear of the LORD are riches, and honor, and life.

When the Apostle Peter tells us to teach rhetoric (or debate) in our high school classes (1 Pet. 3:15), he doesn't spend much time dealing with method. How might one go about preparing "to give an answer for the hope that is within you"? The Greek thinker Aristotle provided a full 300-page textbook on the subject of rhetoric, but he forgot to mention the two indispensable elements that must be part of every rhetoric class. Peter would never think of teaching rhetoric to teenagers without "humility and fear." Thus, you can see that the fisherman stands in radical opposition to the philosopher. They propose two radically different forms of education.

But the schools still believe that you can be successful without humility and the fear of God. They are busy "raising tomorrow's leaders." That is the overused byline touted by public high schools in Colorado—as if everybody gets to be "the leader"! Pride in human achievement and self-assurance constitute the very backbone of modern education. It would be against the law to fear God or to teach the fear of God in those classrooms. So are these riches and honor that they seek after anything but fleeting things? It is interesting that the most proud and wealthy nations in our day are those that have incurred the most debt! Americans live in homes twice the size of houses built one hundred years ago (on average), and their household debt is twenty times what it was then (adjusted for inflation)! They are proud. They live beyond their means. But they are far more impoverished and enslaved than they ever were! What would have happened to this nation if the schools had trained young people to be humble and to tremble before God in their biology laboratories during all those years? They would have had true riches, honor, and life that extended through the generations. There would have been some inheritance to pass on to the next generation. Instead, now only 5% of Americans will receive anything substantial in the form of an inheritance from their parents.

Family Discussion Questions:

1. What are some of the general patterns by which God works in history? How can this help us to predict what will happen in the future?

2. How does Peter's view of rhetoric differ from Aristotle's?

3. If a nation neglects humility and the fear of God in their classrooms, will it be a truly wealthy nation? Why or why not?

PART 187 ~ DESTRUCTIVE PEOPLE AND TRAINING CHILDREN
Proverbs 22:5

Thorns and snares are in the way of the froward: he that does keep his soul shall be far from them.

The characters in real life are not always that different from those we find in children's fictional stories. There are both "good guys" and "bad guys" in the true story that makes up our lives. In some sense, we are all by nature "bad guys," but God's redeeming grace restores us and renews every aspect of our broken-down lives. But there are still those who break things down. They ruin relationships. They trounce on churches and destroy families. They can even destroy entire economies.

But how would you recognize one of these "perverse" men should you run into one? When a couple of children work for hours building a castle out of blocks, a perverse child delights himself in kicking it over and stomping on it. He enjoys torturing animals or invading the privacy of others while they dress. As the froward child turns into a man, his perversity becomes more sophisticated. Following the example of the Marquis de Sade, he looks for the most heinous ways in which he might break the seventh commandment, "Thou shalt not commit adultery." It would not be safe to live near this man because of the sorts of things he might do to our wives and children. In the business world, this man is consummately dishonest and uncooperative. The quicker you can identify these men and avoid them, the better for all around them.

To watch a close relative spiral into sexual rebellion, spousal abuse, divorce, loss of employment, and even criminal behavior is often painful. Short of government welfare programs, these men would quickly die in a ditch somewhere, drunk and destitute. But the most important thing to realize about these froward men is that you cannot fix them, and neither can governments. They are cursed. Thankfully, God can fix them and sometimes He will fix them by the effectual preaching of the Word of God. But if these men and women refuse to hear the preaching and refuse to repent, then the warning still stands: keep your soul far from them!

Proverbs 22:6

Train up a child in the way he should go: and when he is old, he will not depart from it.

A tiny kitten can make an impression on freshly-poured concrete, but even an elephant cannot make a mark on it once it is set. Like hardened concrete, old habits become hard to chip out, and the easiest lessons to learn are those you learn when you are young. Here is the reason why parenting is so crucial to a child's future and to the future of an entire society. While it is possible to "teach an old dog new tricks," it is much easier to work good character into the life of a child when he is young.

Some habits have less spiritual import than others. If a child is trained to brush his teeth every day for 7,250 days until he is eighteen years old, he will most likely brush his teeth on a daily basis for the rest of his life. But this lesson applies to much more than brushing teeth. Generally, a child who is raised in the nurture and admonition of the Lord will not depart from it (Eph. 6:4). Nowadays, parents are not always consistent in this training. Thus, the children pick up on a double-mindedness within the family. When Dad wanted to come home early from the church worship service in order to catch the Super Bowl game, what might he have communicated to his children? Perhaps God was important to the father and mother at points. But with this kind of inconsistency in the home, some of the children may have caught the vision for the kingdom of God, while others might retain a worldly vision. Moreover, education and training is usually not limited to what children receive from their parents. Often, children from Christian homes are raised and influenced more by their peers, neighborhood friends, and day school teachers than they are by their parents. Their culture is far more defined by these sources than by their own parents because they spend far more time, in aggregate, with these people than they do with their own parents. Over time, the children's affections and allegiances are more attached to the ideas and culture of the world, than to the faith-commitments held to by their parents.

Some children learn the way of faithlessness in the home. By example, their parents showed them how to be anxious, how to worry, and how to doubt the grace of God. During days of crisis, these parents would doubt God's ability to provide, or even His ability to save their own children. They would not turn to the Lord in prayer and supplication with thanksgiving, making their requests known unto God (Phil. 4:5–7). And their children watched the whole thing and walked in the ways of faithlessness.

Then there are those children raised in pride and presumption, always presuming on the grace of God. Their parents would not faithfully and carefully admonish, exhort, rebuke, and warn their children as we see with the father exemplified in the Book of Proverbs. Perhaps these parents were content with a mere profession of faith, a baptism, or a confirmation. Whatever the case, their children learned the lesson well— that they may presume on the grace of God. They never learn that the Christian life is filled with things like repentance, mortification of sin, cutting off right arms, and plucking out right eyes.

At the end of the day, whatever faith and character our children have is a matter of the grace of God. But it is for us to work out that salvation with fear and trembling. It is for us to teach the lessons of faith and humble faithfulness by our own example, and rely on the grace of God to bring about their salvation.

Family Discussion Questions:

1. How would you describe a perverse (or froward) child or man?

2. How do you fix a froward man?

3. Who is raising our children? From whom do they learn their habits, their speech patterns, their music tastes, etc.?

4. What are we teaching our children? Do we teach them to trust in God or to fear man?

PART 188 ~ DEBT SLAVERY
Proverbs 22:7

The rich rules over the poor, and the borrower is servant to the lender.

The richest nation in the world does not believe this proverb because the richest nation in the world is fast becoming the largest debtor in the world. Regardless of what the smooth-tongued gods of the marketplace might tell you, debtors are impoverished. Debt is a cursed state. It is among the list of curses God places on disobedient, wicked nations (Deut. 27–28). Should a poor brother in the church be found to be in debt for his home, it would be wrong to despise such a one. But neither is it wise to praise him for his debt. This is not a desirable state; it is a state of bondage, and Deuteronomy 15 would limit this enslavement to no more than seven years. God's people should not be perpetually enslaved by thirty-year loans and the like. The Apostle Paul uses stronger language in 1 Corinthians 7:21–23. "You are bought with a price, be not the servants of men!" he says. If Christ is the Son of God Who redeemed us by His blood, then that redemption extends to our enslavement to banks, corporations, and governments.

Why would any Christian desire debt bondage when he has been redeemed from that bondage by the precious blood of Jesus Christ? These are hard words for a decadent society that lives with twenty times more debt slavery per household than it did in 1900! If you can be free from the unnecessary servitude of men, Paul says, "Use it rather."

This little verse stands against most of the world economies today that were built on the Keynesian Debt Model. Almost every developed nation now has adopted this economic system, assuming that they will retain their economic and political strength with that debt. Will this little verse be found to be true in the end? As always, time is the great "teller." Against this colossal lie formulated by John Maynard Keynes—a lie that has deceived the greatest economies in the world—the truth will one day vindicate itself. Now I hope you can see how the wisdom from the Book of Proverbs will prove to be of the utmost importance for those who would humbly submit themselves to it. Should Christ tarry and the world continue into future centuries, the one-hundred-year experiment with Keynesian economics will serve as another powerful illustration of this potent little principle.

But how is it that the rich rule over the poor? Democratic governments give the poor the illusion that they hold equal power in elections. Yet even in these nations there are always a few rich people who own the media and control the schools. The political agenda of these nations is very much controlled by these institutions. In this country, powerful left-wing foundations such as the Carnegie Foundation, the Gates Foundation, and the Rockefeller Foundation have funded social planning organizations, media campaigns for liberal causes, and education grants. During the first part of the 21st century, wealthy homosexuals flooded monies into numerous political campaigns to secure control over a number of state governments in this country. When it takes one hundred million dollars to win a gubernatorial campaign, you know that the poor have little to do with the political outcome of these elections. One way or another, the rich always rule over the poor.

Proverbs 22:8

He that sows iniquity shall reap vanity: and the rod of his anger shall
fail.

It is a principle that never fails: "Whatsoever a man sows that
shall he also reap. For he that sows to his flesh shall of the
flesh reap corruption; but he that sows to the Spirit, shall
of the Spirit reap life everlasting" (Gal. 6:7–8). Sometimes
young men will leave home, join the military, and waste their
youth on fornication and drunkenness. As the years go by,
they will always suffer the consequences for these things—
always! By their early forties, they deal with cirrhosis of the
liver and sexually transmitted diseases. Those who persist in
the adulterous lifestyle of fornication and divorce are saddled
with alimony, endless court battles over their children, and
the pain of broken relationships. Contrast this with the young
man who kept himself pure from these destructive sins.
Happily married at twenty-three, by the time he makes his
forties, he finds great delight in a family of nine children and
a faithful, loving wife. How a man chooses to live his life at
the beginning will affect his later years.

Angry men will do what they can to lessen the effects of their
iniquity. They will kick, scream, and force their will upon a
person or situation. By sheer brute force, they look to find a
way or make a way to bring about their agenda. But angry
men are not sovereign over reality, as much as they would
like to control it. Eventually, they will see their power, money,
innovation, and strength fail. Every man who attempts to
compete with God for sovereignty will meet his "Waterloo."

From the outset, powerful men think they can break God's
laws with impunity. They fail to fear God or even to fear
the consequences of their actions as they give way to sexual
perversions. When warned about the AIDS virus, these men
trust rather in science. Confident that scientific technology
will one day solve the problem of AIDS, they cannot believe
that God can possibly beat them at their game. But God's hand
is working through every virus in every cell of their bodies—

and He is absolutely thorough in both His knowledge and His judgment concerning every situation on earth. Nothing can possibly "slip through the cracks" as the mills of God grind slowly and very, very finely.

Family Discussion Questions:

1. What does the Bible say about debt? Is it a sin? Is it a desirable condition? How does this compare with what the average person thinks about debt?

2. How is it that the rich rule over the poor even in democracies?

3. What are you sowing now? What will you expect to reap?

4. What is anger? Reference James 4:1–3.

PART 189 ~ THE CHARITABLE SOUL AND THE CONTENTIOUS SOUL
Proverbs 22:9

He that has a bountiful eye shall be blessed; for he gives of his bread to the poor.

The bountiful eye is a man who has an eye for charity. He looks for the opportunity to help others. When traveling on the freeway at seventy-five miles per hour, the average person would never be able to stop to help a stranger in need because it would take too long to respond and slow the vehicle down to a full stop. But occasionally there are those who have a mindset for helping others. They are always looking well ahead of them on the road for some stranded motorist. This gives them enough time to slow down, examine the scene, and pull to the side of the road if it appears that they could help. This applies to every situation in life. If you aren't ready and willing to help a widow when you pull into the church parking lot on a Sunday morning, chances are you will not be helping any widows on that day.

How many times do we hear of a woman who was attacked by a gang of thugs, and nobody came to her assistance? There are two reasons for this. First, our people (especially in the big cities) do not have a mindset to go out of their way to help others. But secondly, people always assume that the government should be the only entity responsible for helping others. They don't want to get involved with the wounded man on the side of the road because they think that is the purview of the police or maybe the "Federal Department of Accosted Strangers." This kind of approach to charity is patently unbiblical.

The man in verse 9 is the true "liberal" or bountiful soul. Notice that he gives his bread to the poor. As opposed to the charlatan liberals in our day, this man is much more generous with his own money than he is with "other people's money!"

Proverbs 22:10

Cast out the scorner, and contention shall go out; yea, strife and reproach shall cease.

We cannot countenance contention and strife in our homes and churches. The Bible calls us to peace. If our homes are filled with arguments, yelling, debates, and contention, they are not Spirit-filled homes, for peace is one of the fruits of the Spirit. Our discussions must be laced with a desire both to understand the truth better and to achieve better unity with our brothers and sisters in the process. Hence, we must assume first that we do not have a full grasp of the truth before we engage with a brother who has a slightly different perspective. Yet this presupposition is not shared by the scorner. He rejects the possibility that anybody has something to add to his great store of wisdom. That is why he cannot be a player in the discussions. Unless he repents of his proud arrogance, he cannot participate in our discipleship centers, schools, churches, and homes.

Family Discussion Questions:

1. How does government discourage the impulse to engage in personal charity?

2. What is a bountiful eye? Do we have this in our home?

3. What is a scorner, and why does he contribute to contention in a home?

PART 190 ~ PURENESS OF HEART AND TRUTH
Proverbs 22:11

He that loves pureness of heart, for the grace of his lips the king shall be his friend.

A glass of water with dirt in it is contaminated because it has a foreign substance mixed into it. But if that is impure water, then what is an impure heart? It is the double-minded man who is unstable in all his ways. He seems to have some interest in the kingdom, but he is out for his own interests as well. In his service to the king, this unprincipled man may find some opportunity to make personal gain in a significant way, and then he proceeds to commit an act of treason against the kingdom itself! Perceptive kings or business leaders can usually discern when staff members begin to wane a little in their dedication to the kingdom. It may be that a business group is pressed to work eighteen-hour days for an entire week as they try to make an important deadline. During these critical moments, it is those who are truly dedicated to the project who will stick to the task until it is done. The king's closest friends will be those who are willing to go to the mat for him and for the cause of the kingdom. Of course, our Lord discerns our own hearts better than anybody. He knows exactly when we become a little cold and disinterested toward His kingdom's interests (Matt. 6:33).

The second thing that attracts good leaders is gracious, winsome communication. Typically, no leader appreciates a negative, discouraging, dour report. Good leaders do need to hear about the challenges and difficulties their organizations face except in the context of optimistic, innovative, and promising solutions. Within organizations, there should be an overall sentiment of positive enthusiasm, an expectation of eventual success, and bright hope concerning the future. In some senses, only a true Christian who believes in the final resurrection can exhibit this kind of solid hope and true optimism.

Proverbs 22:12

The eyes of the LORD preserve knowledge, and He overthrows the words of the transgressor.

Falsehood is everywhere. In political races, when the conservative opposes the liberal, does it ever occur to you that both could be equally wrong? Or in the area of economics, when the free market capitalist opposes the communist, what if both parties are committed materialists? As should be obvious from everything you have learned from the Book of Proverbs thus far, God's economic theories are vastly different from those of Karl Marx or John Maynard Keynes! There are thousands of ways to hell, and the hearts of men concoct new heterodoxies every day.

Even those churches that purport to be "Bible" Churches still impose their own theological constructs over Scripture. Occasionally, they will subject the Bible to their own preconceived ideas, and they fail to correctly handle the mysteries of the faith, for no systematic theology could ever perfectly comprehend these mysteries.

So if the churches and the conservatives are incapable of preserving knowledge in the deceived and deceiving hearts of men, will the truth be lost forever? Of course not! God will see to it that His truth is preserved from generation to generation. He preserves His written Word. But without humble hearts to receive that Word, in complete reliance on the Spirit of God to open eyes and enlighten minds, we will lose the truth again.

If heretics like Arius and Pelagius misinterpreted His words, then you can count on the fact that the Lord of the Church will destroy their works as the centuries proceed. For example, Thomas Aquinas admitted all of his works to be nothing but straw. Even so, the humanist renaissance would never have proceeded without these works. Aquinas refused to accept the noetic effects of the fall (the depravity and deceitfulness of the mind), and he separated theology from philosophy (separating divine revelation from special revelation). If his conclusions were truly straw, God will destroy them in His time though He may take 100 or 800 years to destroy them.

Family Discussion Questions:

1. What is a double-minded man?

2. Describe a winsome employee who would be appreciated by his manager.

3. What will happen to the millions of deceptions that are promulgated today?

PART 191 ~ DEALING WITH OBSTACLES AND HARLOTS
Proverbs 22:13

The slothful man says, There is a lion without, I shall be slain in the streets.

Since slothfulness is a primary sin, the Book of Proverbs provides as many marks of this cursed condition as necessary to identify it in any person. And here we find another mark. Because of perceived obstacles in his way, the slothful man will not proceed to his work. As it turns out, real or perceived obstacles are a part of life. Whether they are working with a difficult coworker, making cold calls in a marketing campaign, or working an endless string of bugs out of a computer program, life is filled with many challenges. You can stay awake late at night worrying about the challenges awaiting you in the work place, or you can attack them with an optimistic vigor in the morning. It takes a relentless, steady force to make it through the obstacle course of life.

Somebody once said, "Half of the potential problems we worry about never happen; and half of the problems that do come about, we never bothered to worry about." So does this mean that we are doing the right amount of worrying? While there may or may not be much truth in that statement, it is still important that we address the problems that are real. In the case of the slothful man, his negative view toward the future constantly generates problems in his mind that have little to do with reality. He discourages himself from work by refusing to deal in reality with real, objective problems. It is practically impossible to foresee all of the potential problems, let alone solve all of those problems in a project before addressing yourself to the project. For one thing, imaginary problems are hard to define. Diligent people appreciate problem solving. They are problem solvers. Once they have a real, definable problem, they set out to identify effective solutions to the problem.

Children will learn the form of diligence stressed in this proverb as they confront increasingly difficult lessons while they study mathematics. At some point, the material may become so intimidating that they begin to avoid it entirely. They gripe and complain over the difficulty of the material. They may even rely on their parents or tutors to solve all the most difficult problems for them. But in these sequential programs, it is unwise to move along in the course before the students have comprehended the previously-presented material. So there is only one thing for the child to do. Get a gun, shoot the lion, and go plow the fields! Thus, you can see that diligence is a heart attitude. It is the "can-do" attitude that is committed to getting the job done whatever the cost. Our children should learn these lessons well in their early years if they will effectively address the lion problems in their adult years.

Proverbs 22:14

The mouth of strange women is a deep pit: he that is abhorred of the LORD shall fall therein.

What a strange spell the sensuous harlot casts upon some young men! She draws men into her trap like a moth to a flame or a dust particle to a vacuum cleaner. But some men are able to resist her most tempting wiles. They can see through the temptation to the demonic source of it. It is not that these men are insensitive to attraction. It is just that God has Himself strengthened them from giving in to the thing that could destroy their souls. So the reason that some men are easy prey to the temptress is that the Lord has chosen not to bless them with adequate defenses against her temptations. And the reason He will not bless them is that He finds them abhorrent. These are chilling words. Sometimes we may wonder why a friend or relative is easily taken by the sin of adultery or fornication, and here is the answer. It all leads back to the adulterer's estranged relationship with God Himself. Until that condition is fixed by the electing and regenerating grace of God, sixteen teams of work horses could not keep him out of trouble.

Family Discussion Questions:

1. How do you handle tough problems and obstacles in your life? Do you procrastinate or do you work through your problems?

2. Who is the "strange woman" who is referred to several times in the Proverbs? Why do some men fall into the traps set by this woman?

PART 192 ~ FOOLISH CHILDREN
Proverbs 22:15

Foolishness is bound in the heart of a child; but the rod of correction shall drive it far from him.

Contrary to the teachings of men like Jean-Jacques Rousseau and other romantic writers from the 19th century, the Bible does not teach the innate "innocence" of children. Even many professing Christians, who have heavily imbibed of the Romantic writers, reject the idea that children are innately sinful. But the Bible teaches that the hearts of children are naturally inclined toward "perverting their way" (Prov. 19:3). For their hearts are bound up in foolishness. Left on their own, children would eventually destroy themselves and others—a scenario aptly presented in William Golding's horrible tale, *Lord of the Flies*. Much of the moral and social chaos and revolutions coming out of the last several centuries is very simply a result of children being left to themselves. With the breakdown of parenting during the industrial revolution and its aftermath, parenting became a lost art over successive generations. By 2010, 64% of children under six in this country were "latchkey" status, with both parents working outside of the home. Absent parenting produces a breakdown of character and morality among some, but also precipitates an increase in petty dictatorships, bloody tyrants, and endless bureaucracy.

How does one change the heart of a child? This is the paramount question. Parents know that only God can ultimately change the heart of a person, but, by God's direction, there are also certain things parents can do to make a difference. Teaching the wisdom of God's Word and prayer are obvious. Some refer to these as "means of grace." But this verse adds another "means of grace" to a parent's tool bag in the form of "the rod of correction." But how does the rod save a child from eternal death? Put another way, are there things parents can do to teach a child to be wise, thereby preventing his soul from going to hell? As certainly as the preaching and reading of the Word of God can bring salvation (Rom. 10:14ff), the right use of the rod can do the same. While God is always sovereign over how much corn a farmer will reap, it is fairly certain that farmers will not yield much of a crop if they refuse to plant any seeds! Even so, a parent must faithfully and consistently teach the absolute character of the laws of God to his children by regular teaching and by the use of the rod. And every time the law is taught, it should further establish in the minds of our children the need for God's mercy and forgiveness. The law impresses upon them their need for grace. As they receive God's forgiveness, then they will walk in the way of God's love and keep the very same commandments their parents taught them!

Proverbs 22:16

He that oppresses the poor to increase his riches, and he that gives to the rich, shall surely come to want.

A poor honey farmer in California produced several hundred beehives, which supplied a modest living for his family. Within a few years, he discovered that several large companies were taking subsidies from the government, which enabled them to cut the prices of their honey. This poor farmer soon found himself out of business because he could not possibly sell his honey for a profit while competing with the subsidized farms. Should the government subsidies dry up, prices for these farm products soar. These higher prices will oppress the consumers who rely on these products, especially if there is far less competition as a result of the government intervention.

Presently, the United States federal government distributes a full $20 billion in farm subsidies each year, much of which ends up in the hands of large farms, grain brokers, food processors, and prepackaged food companies rather than small family farms. Research conducted by The Heritage Foundation found that nearly 75% of the subsidy money goes to the top 10% of wealthy recipients. The same effect is seen internationally as well. Throughout the first decade of the 2000s, industrialized nations increased subsidies for agriculture, benefiting the largest companies and land owners. This, in turn, worked to destroy the livelihoods of poor farmers in developing countries.

Of course, these policies oppress the poor and drive them into perpetual poverty and enslavement to corporations. But they are worse than that. These policies destroy the basic motivations that provide for an all-around healthy economy, free market competition, small businesses, an upwardly mobile middle class, and so forth. In the end, this will drive the corporations themselves into bankruptcy and bring a one-time thriving economy to its knees.

Family Discussion Questions:

1. What are the best ways to drive foolishness from the heart of a child?

2. How does the rod teach the law of God and lead our children to God's salvation?

3. How do government subsidies oppress the poor?

PART 193 ~ A BRIEF INTERLUDE— ARE YOU LISTENING?
Proverbs 22:17–21

Bow down your ear, and hear the words of the wise, and apply your heart unto my knowledge.
For it is a pleasant thing if you keep them within you; they shall withal be fitted in your lips.
That your trust may be in the LORD, I have made known to you this day, even to you.
Have not I written to you excellent things in counsels and knowledge that I might make you know the certainty of the words of truth;
that you might answer the words of truth to them that send unto you?

Here the father interrupts his instructions in wisdom for a brief personal exhortation. As fathers teach their children the wisdom of the Word, it is appropriate from time to time for a little exhortation on *listening!* Every preacher worth his salt will look up occasionally from his notes and make sure everybody is still paying attention. Always reaffirming the importance of the words communicated, he makes sure that his listeners understand the goal of the teaching.

Good listening does not come naturally. How often do your thoughts wander as your father or mother teaches you the words of wisdom? You see, you must apply yourself to the words of wisdom. It does take discipline to stay tuned into good teaching. You have to believe that what you are hearing is important and that it may save your life at some point. Suppose that you were a soldier preparing to raid the enemy camp. Your captain is outlining three things you need to know that will make the difference between life and death in this raid. Do you think that you would pay close attention to what he has to say? You might repeat the words silently in your mind. Or you may write them down on note paper. Now what would you say about some young soldier who was playing a hand-held electronic game while the Captain gave his critical orders? Why is he so disinterested in the Captain's words? For one thing, he has failed to soberly and gravely consider the life-and-death circumstances facing him. But the arrogance to think that there is nothing to learn from a wise counselor in the most important matters of life is nothing short of deadly. Perhaps you might tell this young man, "Listen to the Captain. Humble yourself. Listen to him or die." *Bow down your ear, and hear the words of the wise, and apply your heart unto my knowledge.*

The wise father in the Proverbs shares his goals with his young disciple. All of these efforts in teaching his son are geared to bring him to trust in the Lord, speak and act in wisdom, and disciple others in the words of truth. Faith is foundational in the life of the saint. Faith is of essence. Without faith, it is impossible to please God. Without faith, there is no life. Without faith, there is no freedom in the forgiveness of our Lord. Without faith, there are only guilt-consumed, merit-based, slave-minded works. But how do all of these law-oriented principles generate a trust in the Lord? Well, of course, the Bible never separates the law of God from the comfort of God's sovereign salvation in Christ. And it is only by God's power that we will ever be able to implement any of these principles in any meaningful way! Every law in the Old Testament and every principle given in the Book of Proverbs for the discipleship of our children presumes the prerequisite of faith. Don't even try to read these commands in this book, or execute them, without faith!

Our children need to understand that the vast majority of the world still has not heard the truth—even the truths which they have learned from this little Book of Proverbs. The world is lost in blindness, deceived by billions of various deluding books, magazines, newspapers, videos, and teachings. So if you have any knowledge of the truth, how can you sit passively by while so many others have never heard it? Of course, some willfully reject the truth; they have no interest in it. But the fields are always white. There are those who would be delighted to hear the Word of truth, and their ears are open to it (by God's good purposes). Therefore, it is not for the Christian to fill his head with wonderful notions of truth and then never really do anything with them! God is not interested in fat-headed slugs populating His kingdom! If, by the grace of God, you have come to the knowledge of truth, go share it with somebody.

Family Discussion Questions:

1. Why are we teaching the Book of Proverbs to our children? What are the goals of this teaching?

2. How well are you listening to these words? What have you learned thus far in this series of studies?

3. If you have learned some good things from God's Word, what should you do now?

PART 194 ~ ROBBING THE POOR
Proverbs 22:22–23

Rob not the poor, because he is poor: neither oppress the afflicted in the gate:
For the LORD will plead their cause, and spoil the soul of those that spoiled them.

Most reasonable people would never commend the robbing of the poor. But the robbing of the poor happens all the time. Even the shyster who sells his useless trinkets and snake oil remedies to the impressionable poor will lie to himself about what he is doing. He will never admit that he is out to rob the poor. But he sells them things that they do not need, often for prices that exceed the market value of the product. This kind of marketing is robbery, plain and simple.

But the proverb applies as much to the institutional systems as it does to individuals. The celebrated patron saint of the 20th century was a woman named Margaret Sanger, the founder of the organization called Planned Parenthood. She is touted as the savior of the poor in the American inner cities, as well as billions of others in Asia, Africa, and South America. This woman's influence over the entire globe is simply staggering. Over fifty years of dedicated hard work, she fought for birth control and the development of the birth control pill. In a remarkably honest moment, Sanger once wrote, "The most merciful thing that a family does to one of its infant members is to kill it." To this day, the Planned Parenthood organization certifies its love for mankind with the slogan, "Every child a wanted child." But God defines love by His commandments. When men define love on their own terms, they embody the words of that proverb which says, "The tender mercies of the wicked are cruel."

The effects of Sanger's work are simply breathtaking. One hundred years after she began her work, at least eighty nations around the world are birth imploding, and there were less children in the world in 2010 than there were in 2000. This woman may very well have produced the largest international demographic shift since the worldwide flood. Recently, scientists studying the wombs of women who took Sanger's birth control pills discovered partially embedded fetuses covered by scar tissue in the endometrium of the uterus. Unwittingly, hundreds of millions of women who have taken the pill had no idea that their wombs would become graveyards for perhaps billions of dead babies.

God is particularly concerned about how we handle the poor, and the hypocritical "liberals" that refused to define "love" by the laws of God will face His righteous judgment. The legacy of people like Margaret Sanger will die a miserable death in the next century or two. Over time, people will come to realize the horrible curses these wicked systems brought upon our nation. They will see the terrible effects of the billions and billions of dollars of tax monies that funded Planned Parenthood through the latter half of the 20th century. With unrelenting force, the words of Yahweh in Exodus 22:22–24 will fall upon and slay those nations that "helped" the poor by killing them:

"If you afflict [the fatherless and widow] in any wise, and they cry at all unto me, I will surely hear their cry; And my wrath shall wax hot, and I will kill you with the sword; and your wives shall be widows, and your children fatherless."

Family Discussion Questions:

1. How does an individual shyster rob the poor? In what sorts of ways do large institutions commit this sin?

2. How did the work of Margaret Sanger oppress the poor?

PART 195 ~ THE ANGRY MAN
Proverbs 22:24–25

Make no friendship with an angry man; and with a furious man you shall not go:
Lest you learn his ways, and get a snare to your soul.

Particular sins come to characterize some men, and here the wise father again warns his son of the man characterized by sinful anger. This is the man who creates tension in his home—constantly. Everybody is on pins and needles nearly all of the time. They're never sure when this fellow is going to blow his top. He is the control freak, trying to be sovereign, but becomes frustrated when he can't pull it off. He rules by brute force. He will make everything go his way by forcing his agenda on the hapless souls who happen to live in his household.

Thus, angry men who will not repent of their sin of anger have no place in the church of Christ. We cannot allow them to upset our fellowships because they do not exhibit the humility of repentance. This is not to say that the church requires sinless perfection. But without a life of sincere repentance, the church of Christ would be destroyed by this kind of leaven.

What do you do about the poor family, though, that is cursed to live under the angry tyrant who refuses to repent of his wickedness? Should the anger erupt into serious violence, the civil magistrate has a duty to act, and a wife should protect herself and her children from real and present threats to life and health. In some cases, it may be prudent for teen-aged children to seek emancipation and move into a more godly environment. Nevertheless, any decision of this sort should only be made in counsel with wise, mature church elders.

Proverbs 22:26–27

Be not one of them that strike hands, or of them that are sureties for debts.

If you have nothing to pay, why should he take away your bed from under you?

A biblical economy is very different from the economic systems in the wealthiest nations in the world today. And the average person on the street would see these words as out-of-date and even preposterous. For this little lesson calls into question most partnerships, corporations, stocks, bonds, mortgages, and all forms of debt. While he recognizes that other people will resort to debt, the wise father counsels his son not to share in that debt.

The United States federal debt grew from 10% of the GDP in 1900 to almost 100% of the GDP in 2010. As mentioned earlier, America's total household debt as a percentage of the GDP is about twenty times what it was in 1900. It is true that these large empires would never have enjoyed so much prosperity, or provided some reprieve from economic depressions, without debt. But the debt only delays the inevitable. As this proverb tells us, if you hang your economic well-being on debt, eventually somebody will come and take away your bed. Or, worse yet, if your entire economy hangs on debt, somebody may come and take away your nation, jobs, wealth, and freedoms.

You can see how this proverb would come across as strange and unworkable in the present day. But the sooner families teach their children these truths, the better they will be protected during difficult economic times. In the years to come, we may have to return to a simpler life that embraces debt-free living and separates from debt-based corporations and banks.

Family Discussion Questions:

1. What should the church do with an angry man who seeks to be in fellowship with the body?

2. What is the difference between sinless perfection and a life of repentance?

3. Is it possible to remove yourself entirely from an economy that runs on debt? How might you seek debt-free living?

PART 196 ~ PROPERTY RIGHTS AND INFLUENTIAL MEN
Proverbs 22:28
Remove not the ancient landmark, which your fathers have set.

Against the Marxist idea of property held in community, private property is basic to a biblical economy. Fundamentally, Marxism sets itself against the family, and that is why the family disintegrated in most of the developed world between 1840 and 2010. The basis for property rights is found in two principles—the eighth commandment and the family unit. Even in the tenth commandment, we are not to covet our neighbor's wife, property, and labor. It is plainly assumed that each neighbor is part of a family unit. Before we even discuss the class envy and the thieving redistribution of the wealth that make up the Marxist doctrine, we should remember that Marxism intends to destroy the sphere of the family. Destroy the family, and you will destroy property rights. Without the family, there is no inheritance to pass on to future generations. Without the family, there can be no private property that stays in the possession of that family unit from generation to generation.

Now you should see how the destruction of private property by the massive growth of government ownership and control over all property in developed countries is tied to the destruction of the family. Since 1900 the family has almost completely disintegrated in the West. In the first settlement at Plymouth Colony, the divorce rate stayed at 0.1% for at least sixty years. Now half of our marriages end in divorce. The number of couples living together outside the bonds of marriage increased thirteen fold from 1970 to 2010, and the nuclear family now makes up less than half of American households.

For the first two years of their settlement, the Plymouth Separatists experimented with communal property. Quickly, they discovered that this led to "a kind of slavery" and slothfulness. Each family was then allotted twenty acres, and according to Governor Bradford, "This had very good success, for it made all hands very industrious so as much more corn was planted than otherwise would have been by any means the governor or any other could use."[6] Farther north in Connecticut, the Fundamental Orders of Connecticut were put in place in June of 1639, guaranteeing the legal protection of each family's property rights, referred to as "allotments of inheritance."

This passage calls into question the role of eminent domain. Does a government have a right to confiscate a man's vineyard or business to provide for a public highway or other important public project? If a thousand people owning the properties between two cities did not all agree to build a road connecting the cities, there is no way that such a road would ever be built. Thus, in order to build modern empires with transportation systems, it would be impossible to do so without access to everybody's property. So governments provide what they consider to be "fair market compensation" for real property and proceed to build their highways and railroads—with or without the consent of the property owners. And they will even exercise the power of eminent domain for private interests and their "important" projects. Men will naturally resort to tyrannical means in order to build their powerful empires and centralized systems. But God condemns this sort of thing. You may remember old King Ahab, who took Naboth's vineyard by force to use for his own purposes. Naboth refused to take

6 William Bradford, *Of Plymouth Plantation* (Boerne: Mantle Ministries, 1998)

compensation for it because it was an inheritance handed down to him from his fathers.

If God wills it to be so, private air travel may one day enable far more decentralized systems of commerce. Hundreds of small airports in communities everywhere will not require the exercise of eminent domain. There will be less of a need to centralize one national economy by expensive highways built by violating private property rights. Decentralized family economies will replace the large corporations that violated private property rights in order to build what were supposed to be vibrant, free economies. But they were never free economies, for they were always controlled, regulated, and even owned by governments. The technology that accommodated tyrannies can do the same thing for freedom. It is just a question of whether men's hearts will return to the socio-economic system designed by the wisdom of God, the Creator of the world.

In the 1930s, there were 7,000,000 family farms operating in America. Now, eighty years later, there are only 500,000 family farms left where the family lives off the proceeds of the farm. There is little fathers have to teach their sons anymore, and very little industrial capital or trade skills pass from generation to generation, from father to son. Such is the plight of the modern family. In order to correctly appreciate the principle contained in this proverb, men must once again root themselves in a local area, instead of wandering from city to city like vagabonds. As young men are mentored by their fathers in a family business, trade, or certain life skills, they will be more likely to embrace the inheritance of their fathers and root themselves in decentralized communities. Then once again the ancient landmarks, businesses, cultural art forms, and agricultural endeavors of their fathers will be treasured by sons and grandsons.

Proverbs 22:29

See a man diligent in his business? He shall stand before kings; he shall not stand before mean men.

A busy man is an influential man. But we must be careful not to conclude that every man who has learned the lesson of diligence understands the more basic principles of life, such as Proverbs 1:7, for example. There are some very busy tyrants who kill more babies in abortion clinics than their competitors do. It is possible that the tyrannical kings like Herod, Ahab, and the Pharaoh were industrious men. While diligence is a commendable character trait, it is not the only character trait, nor is it the most fundamental.

Nevertheless, diligence is necessary to bear influence. So we will train our children to fear God and to be humble and loving, but they also must be diligent in business. What tremendous influence for good can be accomplished by one diligent, God-fearing man!

Family Discussion Questions:

1. How are families, inheritance, and property rights related?

2. What is Marxism, and what are its intentions toward the institution of the family and property rights?

3. What is eminent domain, and how does it interfere with property rights?

4. What is the best way to gain influence in civil government?

PART 197 ~ OVERDOSING ON CHOCOLATE CREAM PIE
Proverbs 23:1–3

When you sit to eat with a ruler, consider diligently what is before you:
and put a knife to your throat, if you be a man given to appetite.
Be not desirous of his dainties: for they are deceitful meat.

Biblical ethics sees no significant difference between the sins of gluttony and drunkenness. Although fundamentalist Christians of the last century have parted from biblical law in this area, God's Word treats both of these as equal forms of the same species of sin. At the present time, there are an estimated one billion people in the world who are overweight, and the problem is getting worse. In this country alone, 70% of its people are overweight, up from 13% in 1970!

For thousands of years, only the wealthiest kings and lords could afford expensive foods. If you were privileged to sit at a rich man's table, you might enjoy a once-in-a-lifetime feast of sumptuous delights. All the way through the 1800s, men and women struggled to put basic foods on the table. Even desserts were fairly uncommon; the average person in America in 1880 consumed five pounds of sugar per year. Now, 120 years later, Americans consume an average of 200 pounds in a year. If this proverb was somewhat relevant to a few people four hundred years ago, how much more relevant it is to every person in every single dining room in America every day of the year!

Whether a man indulges in wine or in chocolate cream pie, he can still fall into the sin of excess. The drunkard hears the plaintive call of another glass of wine, and the glutton hears the call of another piece of chocolate cream pie. Excess is a problem for those who are "given to appetite." Things like food or wine become too important for them, and they find it easy to give in to the temptation. When plates of food are set out at a meal, be aware of your physical and emotional reactions to the food. Are you tempted to take one of each of the desserts, filling your entire plate with sweets? With the massive increase in obesity rates in this country, doctors are predicting a 30% diabetes rate twenty years from now. As a man places too much emphasis on food and goes out of his way to serve his taste buds, he turns food into an idol, and that idol will beat him to death. Idols like this one present themselves as wonderfully beneficent gods, but they always turn out to be cruel and miserable slave masters in the end.

Put a knife to your throat! This warning sounds severe, similar to our Lord Jesus' words in Matthew 5:30, "If your right hand offend you, cut it off." The Christian life calls for self-discipline, which sometimes demands intense severity. If you have never subjected yourself to a self-denial that made you wince a little, you have never really lived the Christian life. This particularly applies to the area of food in the present day since there are a huge number of food choices, and sumptuous delights sold in restaurants on every corner; plenty of money also exists to pay for that food. You had better put a knife to your throat every single day!

Family Discussion Questions:

1. How much more availability of expensive desserts and sweets is there now than there was in the 1700s and 1800s?

2. Where are you tempted to sins of excess? Are there certain sumptuous foods that tempt you into taking an overdose?

3. What are some practical ways in which we might exercise more self-discipline?

PART 198 ~ THE MONEY GOD
Proverbs 23:4–5

Labor not to be rich: cease from your own wisdom. Will you set your eyes upon that which is not?
For riches certainly make themselves wings; they fly away as an eagle toward heaven.

If you turn food into a god it will always disappoint you, and the same principle applies to money. Those who are privileged enough to have saved a little money often count that money to be a source of security for them. They find no further need to trust in God for their daily bread because their retirement savings will keep them for decades—or so they think! Wealth gives men a sense of self-sufficiency. Why do they need God's wisdom to solve their problems for them? Why should they pray to God for their daily provision now? From ancient Israel to modern- day America, this is almost always the way that people handle the blessing of prosperity.

Wealth is a blessing from God. If you work hard and God chooses to give you the blessing of wealth, then you will be wealthy. Though work generally produces wealth, there is no absolute guarantee that this will be the case. Therefore, you should not work in order to be rich. Your chief motivation for work should be to fulfill God's will for your life. From the beginning, God intended men to work so as to take care of the world that He made.

Even if you have enjoyed a bit of wealth as a reward for the work you have done, there is no certainty that your wealth will be sustained. Somebody could sue you for everything you own. Violent revolutions may redistribute the wealth, including yours! Or, some horrible disease may incapacitate a family member, resulting in excessive medical expenses or a loss of income. You should not strive so much for wealth as for contentment. As the Apostle reminds us, "Godliness with contentment is great gain" (1 Tim. 6:6). If you can learn to be equally happy and content with little or plenty, trusting in

God to give you what He wants you to have, then you will be more blessed than every billionaire in the world.

Family Discussion Questions:

1. If God has given us a gift of prosperity, how do we handle it? Do we trust in God for our daily bread?

2. What is the purpose of work? Why should we work?

3. Are we equally happy and content with a little as with a lot? Can we say with Paul, "I have learned in whatsoever state I am, therewith to be content"?

PART 199 ᗌ THE EVIL EYE
Proverbs 23:6–8

Eat not the bread of him that has an evil eye, neither desire his dainty meats: for as he thinks in his heart, so is he:
Eat and drink, says he to you; but his heart is not with you.
The morsel which you have eaten shall you vomit up, and lose your sweet words.

What is this thing called "an evil eye"? We find this several times throughout Scripture, including Matthew 6:23, where Jesus issued the warning, "If your eye be evil, your whole body shall be full of darkness." The eye announces a man's intentions toward something or someone. When a man has an evil eye, he is out for no good, motivated by hatred, greed, covetousness, lust, or envy. This man surveys a woman, and his eye lusts after her. He looks at a neighbor who owns a more elegant home than his own, and he envies his neighbor. He catches a glimpse of a competitor in the marketplace, and his heart is filled with hatred. He is so controlled by envy that you can count on him to sue you on the slightest insult. His heart is so filled with lust that you wouldn't want your daughter alone with him in an elevator for ten seconds.

According to this text, it is very important that we learn to judge the character of those with whom we fellowship and engage in hospitality. If a man is so controlled by lust that he cannot cease from desiring every woman he has ever laid his eyes on, why would you want this man in the presence of your wife or daughters? He has an uncontrollable, consistently immoral eye toward women with whom he has contracted no marital relationship. He would think nothing of taking the virginity of a woman, and he may think nothing of robbing you of your property as well.

If his heart is committed to do evil, no winsome words or sweet complements will win his heart to you. Hard words might be better for him as you point out his sins and call him to repentance. Your words will not be taken as "sweet words" and, without the work of the Holy Spirit transforming his evil eye and wicked heart, he will remain a man with evil intentions toward you and others.

So why does the text warn of accepting favors from this man or taking his "dainty meats"? There is a temptation to resort to superficial standards as we assess a man's character. Even a cannibal has his standards of decency because he daintily wipes his mouth with a banana leaf after consuming human flesh. He may be a generous man, sharing his human meat with his friends. "He's a really nice guy," they say. But is he really a "nice guy"? The most infamous killer of unborn babies in the history of this country was handing out bulletins in the foyer of his Evangelical Lutheran Church in Wichita, Kansas, on the day he met his Maker. If you had met this "nice" fellow handing out the bulletins, you may have assumed purity in his intentions and life. But a minimal inquiry into the man's work and national reputation would have revealed his true character. The wisdom contained here in this proverb is simple—don't be naive! There are evil people in this world who are completely controlled by a commitment to break the laws of God, *and they can do you much harm.* Indeed, they have been known to harm families, churches, and entire communities.

Family Discussion Questions:

1. What is an "evil eye"?

2. How might you determine if somebody has an evil eye? Why is it important for you to make wise judgments concerning the character of others?

PART 200 ∽ PEARLS BEFORE SWINE
Proverbs 23:9

Speak not in the ears of a fool: for he will despise the wisdom of your words.

Some Christian churches are aggressive with what is known as "evangelism," which is a means of communicating words of wisdom to unbelieving neighbors or coworkers. While the Proverbs do compliment the man who "wins souls" (Prov. 11:30), there are also multiple warnings in Scripture concerning "casting pearls before swine." Sadly, this world is filled with fools, or "swine," whose hearts have not been softened to true wisdom.

Be careful not to assume that every person is a fool before you have said anything at all to him concerning God's way of faith and repentance. Jesus reminds us that the fields are white unto the harvest, and there are people who are waiting for us to bring them the message of God's truth. So you must speak these words to them, and if they are fools they will reject the truth. Once you have concluded that they are fools, it will do you no good to continue to pursue them. If they reject you in one city, move on to the next as Jesus told his disciples! There are millions of others who have not heard the words of truth and would profit from your witness. Because many of the Western countries are presently in the midst of a two-hundred-year apostasy, you may find more hardness of heart here than anywhere else. But this only means that you will have to cover larger fields in order to find pockets of soil in which the seeds of the Word will germinate.

How many hundreds of hours are wasted by pastors counseling couples who reject their words? So much more of a pastor's time could have been spent with those who would have gladly accepted his wisdom. It is therefore incumbent upon a pastor to judge how his counsel is received. How are they responding? Do they ignore the advice? Do they change the subject whenever he brings out the real sin issues in their lives? Do they respond in anger? Or do they play the blame game, blaming everybody else for their sins? These are all indications that these folks despise the words they hear from their pastor counselor.

Family Discussion Questions:

1. What do you think is the reason for the severe hardening of hearts in Western nations during the 20th and 21st centuries?

2. What would be good indications that you are wasting your time and speaking to a fool?

PART 201 ~ A MAN'S HOME IS HIS CASTLE
Proverbs 23:10–11

*Remove not the old landmark; and enter not into the fields of the
    fatherless:*
For their redeemer is mighty; He shall plead their cause with you.

The maxim "A man's home is his castle" embodies one of the oldest and most sacred principles of Anglo-American jurisprudence. The greatest English statesman of the 18th century, William Pitt, famously wrote, "The poorest man may in his cottage bid defiance to all the forces of the crown. It may be frail; its roof may shake; the wind may blow through it; the storm may enter; the rain may enter; but the King of England cannot enter—all his force dares not cross the threshold of the ruined tenement!"

The principle contained in this proverb is the basis for the fourth amendment in the American Bill of Rights, and it has prevented many a tyrant from playing out his full intentions in unlawful searches and seizures on millions of innocent citizens! As late as 1880, the Arkansas State Constitution prohibited any confiscation of a widow's property, even if she was not able to pay the taxes due on that property. Thankfully, that document has not yet been modified to eliminate that provision. These sorts of legal protections are just what secured a righteous and free system of government for hundreds of years.

But in 2005 a private development company wrested a piece of real property away from a lone woman named Susette Kelo for the purpose of constructing a hotel, retail, and condominium complex. The city of New London took the side of the big developer. They sued Susette and the case was finally decided by the Supreme Court of the United States against the widow. Do you think that God is mighty enough to oppose the highest court in the most powerful empire in the world? The rest of the story is even more interesting. Originally, the city that brought the suit against Susette had argued that this development would provide more economic vitality and tax revenues to the area. But five years later the project was dead! The company that promised the jobs and economic growth pulled out of the area, taking 1,500 jobs with it (instead of adding the 3,169 jobs they had promised at the beginning of the suit). The violation of a poor woman's rights was all in the name of the "greater good." In this case, "the greater good" never materialized, and the city of New London ultimately lost the case in the courts of heaven.[7] God is never on the side of tyrants, whether it be the city of New London or in the city of King Ahab of the Old Testament.

Family Discussion Questions:

1. What did King Ahab do to violate the principle contained in this proverb?

2. How do modern countries violate this principle?

6 Kelo vs. City of New London, http://en.wikipedia.org/wiki/Kelo_v._City_of_New_London

3. What will God do for those poor people who are tyrannized by powerful governments?

PART 202 ~ INSTRUCTING A CHILD, CORRECTING A CHILD
Proverbs 23:12

Apply your heart unto instruction, and your ears to the words of knowledge.

How many times has the father in this book cried out to his son to apply his heart to instruction, knowledge, and wisdom? It is interesting that the Book of Proverbs does not address the matter of God's regenerating power that opens the heart and ears of those who listen to the Word. Yet, we know that this is the difference between a son and a scoffer. Every appeal like the one in this verse presumes a responsibility on those that listen to the Word. Working out our salvation with fear and trembling involves God working in us to do His good pleasure (Phil 2:12–13). Even so, we open our hearts to the Word of God because God the Holy Spirit opens our hearts, ears, and eyes that we might hear His good will for us.

Heart and ears. Attitude and attention. Without a proper attitude toward the instruction and instructor, not much will be learned. And without the discipline to stay attentive to the words communicated, not much will be retained. If a child's heart is not right toward his mother, he will not be inclined to listen to her instruction. Though she may say the most truthful, beautiful words anybody could say, he will reject them because he rejects her. This may be the most common reason why some children fail in the homeschool setting. But the same lesson applies to the teaching of the Word of God. When a person has a chip on his shoulder against God, he will not be all that interested in listening to His messengers or His message. His bias against God always translates into a bias against the message.

Proverbs 23:13–14

Withhold not correction from the child: for if you beat him with the
*   rod, he shall not die.*
You shall beat him with the rod, and shall deliver his soul from hell.

To the modern mind, this may be one of the most offensive verses in all of the Bible. Humanist man is always churning out new "scientific" studies showing that spanking is detrimental to society. "Violence begets violence," they tell us. Of course, these studies are usually conducted within families that are controlled by anger and selfish retributive outbursts. Therefore, it is not as much a matter of violence producing violence as sinful, self-centered anger in parents producing more sinful, self-centered anger in the children.

Another problem with modern psychology is that it presumes the child to be innocent from birth. "It is the parents and the family that corrupt the child," they say. "He would have been fine if he had not picked up all those nasty habits from his parents and siblings!" Can you see how people's presuppositions will affect how they do their scientific studies and the conclusions they draw from them?

The Bible does not regulate the frequency of the use of the rod, nor does it tell us how early to begin using it with a child. Also, some children may require more discipline than others. Should parents neglect to use the rod altogether in the correction of a child, they ignore an important biblical principle. The results of such permissiveness are not pleasant. Within the limits of God's laws (Exod. 21:24; Deut. 25:1–3; Eph. 6:4), a parent is obligated to make some application of the rod.

Finally, the goal of godly discipline is to deliver the child from a worse fate than death. Again, the humanists cannot fathom such a worldview. They cannot believe there might be anything worse than death because they do not fear God or His holy justice. Everybody is going to die, but not everybody is going to suffer the flames of hell fire! What sort of parent who feared God and loved his child would look the other way while his child walked into a burning furnace of fire? To see a child go to hell is a parent's worst nightmare. Wouldn't he do all within his power to keep that from happening? Thus, proper child rearing will call for all the proper means at our disposal in order to correct, warn, rebuke, comfort, and teach our children in the ways of the Lord. The use of the rod is only one of those means, and it ought to be properly balanced with careful teaching and loving admonition. As covered earlier in the previous chapter (Prov. 22:15), the rod is a preacher. When attended with good teaching, it preaches a good message which is a means whereby God ministers His salvation to the hearts of our children. Children who don't get spanked and never hear a message of God's law and His redemption will most likely go to hell. It would be well, therefore, for parents to take this wise counsel. They should discipline, not in fear, but in faith that God is the rewarder of those who diligently seek Him in the final salvation of their children (Heb. 11:6).

Family Discussion Questions:

1. What two things must a child possess during times of biblical instruction in order to make it a profitable time?

2. How might a child's attitude be corrupted as he comes to family worship to hear the Word of God?

3. What is the purpose of the rod in biblical correction?

4. What are the biblical limits to parental correction?

PART 203 ~ ARE YOU PROUD OF YOUR CHILDREN?
Proverbs 23:15

My son, if your heart be wise, my heart shall rejoice, even mine. Yea, my reins shall rejoice, when your lips speak right things.

Here is a father who loves his son. References to "hearts" and "reins" or "kidneys" in the Old Testament speak of affection deeply-seated in the heart. You can see that the father in this verse has wrapped up a great deal of his own life in his son. Likewise, it is important that our children know that we care about them. But why do we care about them? Do we enjoy their company? Do we take special pride in their academic or physical accomplishments? Or do we desire something even better for them? Much of our love for our children is tainted by selfishness and pride. But the most selfless and loving father will desire wisdom and a right relationship with God for his son. Indeed, there are no greater blessings a father could desire for his children than wisdom and righteousness.

What a blessing it is to hear our children speak wise and kind words to others! When a young man is able to witness the words of truth to others, when he gives a wrathful man a gentle response, when he blesses those who curse him, or when he speaks soberly to a wayward friend, a father's heart leaps for joy!

What a godly father desires more than anything is a wise son who speaks wise words. It is important for a father to desire this for his son, because when a man desires something, he generally gets the thing that is desired. If a man desires to be rich, he will quite often accomplish this goal, but at the expense of other priorities. Usually, when a man desires to have a wise son, he will do everything in his power to see to it that his son learns wisdom. And, more often than not, this will yield a wise son.

Family Discussion Questions:

1. Many people are "proud of their children." Is this appropriate?

2. What sorts of achievements bring great delight to the hearts of unbelieving parents? What is the proper sense in which we rejoice in our children?

PART 204 ~ FEARING GOD ALL DAY LONG
Proverbs 23:17–18

Let not your heart envy sinners: but be in the fear of the LORD all the day long.

For surely there is an end; and your expectation shall not be cut off.

During the last few decades of the 20th century, hundreds of millions of people have turned a fictional character named James Bond into the quintessential screen hero. In the pretend world of motion pictures, he was a British spy who was supposed to defend his nation from malevolent enemies of the state. He was suave, courageous, and apparently impervious to harm. But he was also a promiscuous fornicator and adulterer. He lived "above" morality. He made up his own rules as he went and usually ignored the rules placed upon him by his superiors. It would be hard to estimate how many millions of men and boys envied this lecherous, god-like screen character over the last fifty years. Many Americans can still remember Bond's favorite martini drink: on the rocks, "shaken, not stirred." The softening of an entire nation toward extra-marital fornication certainly required the classy, suave leadership of characters like James Bond and the actors who played the part. But the Bible speaks clearly to the issue of fornication when it tells us that "neither fornicators, nor idolaters, nor adulterers, nor effeminate, nor abusers of themselves with mankind, nor thieves, nor covetous, nor drunkards, nor revilers, nor extortioners, shall inherit the kingdom of God" (1 Cor. 6:9–10).

How are people so easily drawn to these ungodly heroes who obviously do not fear God or His fearsome judgment? It has to be that they have ceased to walk in the fear of the Lord all the day long. Should a child see nothing of his mother for five days, he will soon behave as though his mother was not there. She may have been a good disciplinarian—watching him and correcting him on a regular basis—but without her presence, he begins to act without the "fear of mom." Even so, the farther men live apart from God (in their consciousness), the more they act as if God is not present. They do not take His law seriously. They cannot believe that He will judge them for their crimes, and they encourage others to join them in their disregard for the laws of God.

"Come, ye children, hearken unto me: I will teach you the fear of the LORD."

Psalm 34:11

Learning to fear God as He should be feared comes with a great deal of hard work. It is a process that involves the integration of God-centered teaching into a child's life from early years. To send children to schools where they do not fear God all day long has proven to be a fatal mistake for millions of Christians. Perhaps God is sort of feared on Sunday, but the child is then taught in the science or history class that he does not need to fear God Monday through Saturday. This is why it is so unnatural for many Christians to discern the godlessness of James Bond or a biology textbook. They have learned to fear God a little on Sunday, but this does not permeate their lives the rest of the week.

Now what is the poor Christian to do who looks at worldly men and sees them enjoying themselves in their sins, while he must trudge down the old Pilgrim Pathway full of snares and trials? The wise man here points out the inevitable final end to all things. Even the ungodly have a common saying reminding them that "all good things must end." Everybody knows that there is an end to the party, and there is an end to life. It is called "death." Some of the ungodly may have some tiny, fleeting hope that there may be something good for them on the other side of the tomb. But for those who fear God and believe His revelation in Christ, there is a solid hope and expectation beyond the pain, agony, and death of the present age. The more one fears God, the more he must believe His revelation, the more he must know that God is true to His Word, and the more he knows that all of his expectations and hopes will not fail. Surely, the only way to live life is by the fear of God.

Proverbs 23:19

Hear my son, and be wise, and guide your heart in the way.

"Follow your heart!" How many times have we heard that phrase repeated by the pop psychologists and media of the present age? If it is true that the heart is "deceitful above all things and desperately wicked" (Jer. 17:9), then the heart is hardly worth following. There is, therefore, only one thing you can do—teach your heart with the godly instruction of your father. Your heart must be trained what to think and how to react to what goes on around you. The heart is not a blank slate, as men like John Locke, Aristotle, and Aquinas believed, nor does the human heart naturally tend toward what is righteous and wise from the beginning. Following your heart will always result in disaster. Instead, submit to the teaching of your parents.

The vast majority of children in the world never learn the lessons of the Proverbs or the Psalms (in any comprehensive way). According to one pollster, only 5% of children belonging to "born again" parents have ever heard of family devotions. It may be only one child in 10,000 who receives careful, daily instruction from the Word of God from loving, godly parents who are committed to the Deuteronomy 6:7 and Ephesians 6:4 mandates. And these statistics are from one of the most "Christianized" nations in the world. So what do these few privileged children who receive daily instruction from the Word of God do with the words that they hear? Do they take the words and hide them in their hearts? Do they instruct their own hearts in the proper way to think and live? Or do they reject these words? Children, be careful never to take lightly the precious instruction your parents have given you in God's Word!

Family Discussion Questions:

1. Do characters like James Bond fear God? Why or why not?

2. How do we forget the fear of God? How do we learn the fear of God?

3. What is our greatest hope? What do most ungodly people hope for out of life?

4. What is wrong with the phrase, "Follow your heart"?

PART 205 ~ ASSOCIATING WITH GLUTTONS AND DRUNKARDS
Proverbs 23:20–21

Be not among winebibbers; among riotous eaters of flesh:
For the drunkard and the glutton shall come to poverty: and drowsiness shall clothe a man with rags.

Gluttonous people generally attract other gluttonous people. They attend the same churches, play in the same bingo games, go to the same gambling halls, and live together in the same homes. People are communal, and they tend to rub off on each other. Just as alcoholic parents often produce children who have problems with alcohol, families who have trouble with gluttony will produce more children who have trouble with gluttony. While there may be households that are given to wine and overeating, thank God that there are also repenting households! When a family comes to Christ, they will begin to purge the sins that once dominated their lives. They will gather to read God's Word, worship Him together, and bury their gods as Jacob did before his family worshiped God at Bethel.

If you were to study the correlation between income level and obesity in this country, you would find a significant proportion of obese persons belonging to the welfare class. The same thing can be said about those addicted to alcohol. There may be a few rich people who are burning through their wealth as they drink themselves to death, but men and women who live to eat and drink alcohol have given up on work. They may work some, but it is only to earn a little money to stuff more food in their mouths. How sad that people live for physical sensations on the tongue or in the digestive tract! Because these people are more interested in eating than working, they will eventually produce a terrible drag on the economy. Family economies will die first, and then the welfare economies will collapse too.

There are, however, two contributing sources to the problem of poverty which we see identified in this particular proverb. First, there is the problem of over-infatuation with comfort food and drink. But verse 21 also states that "drowsiness shall clothe a man with rags." Undoubtedly, this must refer to a love of physical sleep, the activity that turns a man into a limp rag who is hardly motivated to do anything. The reason that twenty-five to thirty-year-old young men are the only demographic making less money than they did thirty years ago is that they have lost their motivation and focus. They are out of touch with reality. They have become very, very drowsy. Their lives are made up of popular movies, music, and Internet games, and their true identities are increasingly confused with their online virtual personalities. This presses them into a dream-like state, a pretend world. This phenomenon is repeated in places like Europe, Australia, Japan, South Korea, and China. In a hundred years, billions of people will better understand the force of this truth: drowsiness shall clothe a man with rags.

It is better that a person would sooner live to work than to eat, sleep, or dull his senses by living in pseudo-realities. But Christians do not live to work, and they certainly do not live to eat or to waste time. Neither do they work to eat, in the basic sense. They live, work, and eat all to the glory of God!

Family Discussion Questions:

1. What happens to families in which fathers give way to gluttony or drunkenness? What happens to families in which fathers repent of their sins of gluttony or drunkenness?

2. What are two contributing sources to the problem of poverty?

Part 206 ~ Honor Your Father and Mother
Proverbs 23:22

Hearken [listen] unto your father that begat you, and despise not your mother when she is old.

We are slowly working our way into the very heart of Proverbs. At this point, it would be good to review the purpose of this wonderful book before we proceed to its heart. You may remember that this book is God's curriculum for the education of a child. It presents God's take on subjects like epistemology, metaphysics, ethics, anthropology, human relationships, economics, and government. This book is God's theory of education presented in method and content.

The teacher in the Book of Proverbs is a father. He is not a metaphorical, spiritual, or church father. In the clear text of this verse, he defines himself as the biological father, whose genetic code the child shares. It is on the basis of this relationship that he pleads his case with his son. The father-son relationship means something. It holds weight in the argument. His teaching would lose force without it. He says, "You share my genetic code. You are my son. Now listen to me!" Since the onslaught of the modern economies as early as the 1750s, fathers have been replaced by orphanages, Sunday School teachers, youth group leaders, and day school teachers. These institutions may do some good things, but without a biblical system of child discipleship, they will eventually fail.

This world is filled with great teachers and pastors, but nobody can disciple a child like a parent. There is no more powerful form of discipleship or evangelism than that of a parent who tenderly takes his child by the hand and says, "Let me show you my Savior, the Lord Jesus Christ!" God has hard-wired this into the parent-child relationship. It is His assigned means of kingdom replication. Many evangelicals love to speak of how important it is to "witness to your neighbors," but there isn't much in Scripture that would bind the conscience of every person to witness to his neighbors every day. Some are called to evangelistic ministries, but others are not. Yet every father is called to disciple his children as they sit in the house, as they walk by the way, as they rise up, and as they lie down (Deut. 6:7).

Despise not your mother when she is old. A son is bound to honor his mother until the day she (or he) dies. This honor takes a different form as a child becomes an adult. For example, in 1 Timothy 5:6–8, the Apostle Paul holds a son responsible for the material well-being of his widowed mother. If there is no son to take care of her needs, the responsibility falls to a grandson or to a nephew. Too many elderly people now sit out their failing years in lonely rest homes without any meaningful relationships with children or grandchildren. It has become increasingly rare to find sons who are willing to provide regular care for their mothers who suffer from dementia or something similar, especially when it is clear that these mothers give no economic benefit to those around them. More often than not, this generation would sooner turn the elderly over to social welfare programs than honor them with personal care for their needs. The generation that aborted 100,000,000 of their children shouldn't be surprised to find those who are left of the aborted generation euthanizing the previous generation in return. The treatment of elderly mothers is a sure measurement of how well a society conforms to the laws of God. If a man finds himself having to take care of his parents' incontinence in their old age, he should remember that they changed his diapers when he was unable to take care of himself. Only a faithless ingrate would abandon his mother in her old age.

Family Discussion Questions:

1. Contrast the importance of witnessing to your neighbors versus discipling your children in the Word of God each day.

2. What sorts of things have displaced fatherhood over the last several centuries?

3. How well do families look out for their elderly mothers and grandmothers in the present age? Are we seeing any tendencies toward euthanasia (the killing of the elderly)? How might we provide loving care to our own mothers and grandmothers?

PART 207 ⌒ WISDOM AND RIGHTEOUSNESS FOR OUR CHILDREN
Proverbs 23:23

Buy the truth, and sell it not; also wisdom, and instruction, and understanding.

We buy and sell goods in the marketplace all the time. We may buy stock in a company or purchase a gold coin. Then after a while we turn around and sell the asset for something of greater value or more usefulness to our household economy.

Truth is also an investment! If you are going to invest time and money into something, why not consider the "truth"? If you purchase the truth you never want to sell it again. Hoarding gold may be unwise, even sinful, but hoarding the truth never is! Have you ever known anybody who had something of a grasp on the truth, and then sold it? You may run into a fellow you haven't seen in years, only to discover that he is less familiar with the truth now than he was in his earlier years. How did this happen? Evidently, he found something more attractive than the truth and swapped the truth for the coveted item. To the amazement of his friends and family members, this man, who was once taught the creation story, came to believe that man evolved out of inanimate matter over billions of years. His family may wonder how anybody could ever believe that a rock turned into a human being by a series of chance events! Instead of staying true to his marriage and the proposition that God hates divorce, the man abandoned his wife and moved in with another woman. This story is all too common in the present age, an age of wholesale apostasy in the West. It is one thing for some ignorant pagan to believe in evolution and family-fragmenting divorce, but how much worse is it for somebody who was taught the truth to run headlong into error! It is a thousand times more tragic.

It is one thing to receive the truth, but it is quite another to value, embrace, and hoard it. There are some who have tasted of the heavenly gift, but they refuse to digest it (Heb. 6:4). They never swallowed! So as a father feeds his son wisdom and instruction, he encourages his boy to swallow, digest, and live out the truth.

Proverbs 23:24–25

The father of the righteous shall greatly rejoice: and he that begets a wise child shall have joy of him.
Your father and your mother shall be glad, and she that bare you shall rejoice.

Down in the inner bowels of some large city, a very despondent mother considers the plight of her two sons. As she recovers from broken bones and bruises sustained during a violent conflict with her eldest son, the young man sits in the county jail. Her younger son has a hard time holding down a steady job, mostly due to his recurring drug habit. Contrast this woman with another mother living some twenty miles away whose two sons are wise and righteous men of sterling character. Her older son preaches the Word of God in the inner city, converting drug addicts to a life of faith and holiness. Her younger son uses his engineering skills in a far-off African country to develop water sources that will improve the agriculture of impoverished peoples. His family has lovingly adopted several orphans whose parents died of the AIDS infection. As this kind mother thinks about her two sons, do you think her heart is filled with rejoicing over them? Does she praise God for the work He has wrought in them? Deep within her soul, she experiences a sense of fulfillment in knowing that God has established the work of her hands.

It is important to remind our children how they may be a delight to their father and mother. Parents want to see their children conducting themselves with wisdom and righteousness! Let us be plain about it. Those young men persisting in foolishness and wickedness against the wise counsel of their parents exhibit hatred toward their parents. A child who loves his parents will realize that they invested much of their time, emotions, resources, and energy into him over many years, and the best thing he can do to express his gratitude is to walk in wisdom during his adult years. Naturally, this will only be accomplished if a child loves God first. If a love for God is absent, love for the very closest family relations wanes quickly through the generations.

Family Discussion Questions:

1. How does a young man "sell" the truth? Is this sort of thing common today?

2. What happened to those who tasted of the "heavenly gift" in Hebrews 6:4–6?

3. How might a young man raised in a Christian home exhibit hatred toward his parents? How might he manifest love toward God and toward his parents?

PART 208 ~ THE HEART OF DISCIPLESHIP
Proverbs 23:26

My son, give me your heart, and let your eyes observe my ways.

Finally, we arrive at the very heart of the Book of Proverbs. This book of wisdom emphasizes the importance of relationships in the teaching of a child. If children were computer hard drives, you could stuff facts into their brains and call it "education." But children are made in the image of God and have the capacity for relationship because God has existed in a relationship from all eternity. In contrast to a Christian theory of education, in which this principle is central, the unitarian god of the Muslims and the Humanist Statists is a lonely god and relationships are not a priority. We are not interested in knowledge that is pressed into children through large, heartless institutions. We have little use for a system that herds children through different large classrooms outfitted with a new teacher every year. Children learn best when they are loved by and when they love their teachers.

If the father in this Proverb is to teach his son the most important lessons in life, he must have his son's heart! The relationship of teacher to disciple is vital to the success of the teaching. Yet, it is rare to hear a university professor cry out to his student, "My son, give me your heart!" It is even a little odd for parents to look their child in the eye and say these words. But this is basic to the biblical idea of education, in which we do not separate heart and head. Without the heart, we cannot possibly teach the most important lessons in life. We may try to teach chemistry without teaching the fear of God, or we might attempt to teach a child how to drive a car without teaching him the value of human life. Yet separating education from moral principles, character development, and the fear of God is diametrically opposed to what we have learned in this book thus far. An educator must disciple his young student, and his young student must be willing to give his heart to his teacher in order to be led to true wisdom.

But here it is the father who cries out for his son's heart; he knows that the father-son relationship is the fundamental mentor-disciple relationship. He loves his son. He doesn't want his son going the way of the prostitute! There is alarm in his voice as he cries out these warnings. There is insistence in his voice when he rebukes his son about this sin or that, and there is love when he speaks of his God. If his son is close enough to see his father's heart, he will better see the God Whom his father loves. So the man of faith cries out to his son, "Follow me as I follow God!"

Today, there are powerful forces working to drive a wedge between the hearts of fathers and sons. Overly absorbed in the pursuit of materials, many fathers don't have much time for their little men. Then, as these young sons move into their early teen years, they lose all interest in their fathers' discipleship. They take on the attitudes, habits, music, and culture of a peer group that has been discipled by the pop culture.

In the face of these competing forces, the father charges his son, "My son, give me your heart, and let your eyes observe my ways." Inviting his son into the front row of his life, he gets to the heart of true discipleship. It is more than a lecture from a podium, where the student sits forty feet away from the professor. Instead, the son watches as his father interacts with his subcontractors, his employees, and his customers. He watches as his father faces seemingly insurmountable challenges in his business. He watches his father sin, confess sin, and repent. He watches his father work through conflict in the church community. In the process, he learns one hundred times more than he could ever learn through the best college education available. Relationships allow for powerful, life-integrated learning.

Family Discussion Questions:

1. Why are relationships important to people who believe in the Triune God?

2. Why is it important that the mentor have the heart of his disciple?

3. What are the wedges today that work to separate the hearts of fathers and sons?

4. What is "life-integrated" discipleship or education? Why is this more powerful than a series of lectures given in a large classroom?

PART 209 ~ THE POWERFUL LURE OF THE WHORE
Proverbs 23:27–28

For a whore is a deep ditch; and a strange woman is a narrow pit.
She also lies in wait as for a prey, and increases the transgressors among men.

The lesson contained in these verses is not an easy one to teach. It should not be left to disinterested counselors or "professional" youth leaders. Rather, a father who loves his son is the one who can teach a lesson like this one, but only if the son loves his father, for we are talking about the most insidious, dangerous, and powerful temptations known to man. To neglect a lesson of this import would be akin to allowing a young child to run out into the middle of a busy freeway. So the father cries out to his son, "As you love me, son, listen to me now, because I'm about to warn you about something that could kill you."

Who, then, is the whore spoken of in this passage? To find this woman, a young man must travel to a city or resort to seeking her on the Internet or in a magazine. She is a stranger, a "strange woman," as the father puts it in this proverb. She is making herself up to be somebody that she is not, hiding her real personality behind certain forms of makeup and a care-free, impudent persona. Place a picture of one of these whores next to a picture of an average young woman from the local church who cares to preserve her purity, and you will immediately see stark differences. The whore is more attractive, but only in a sensual way, since she wears her sensuality on the outside for everybody to see. The young virgin from the church is meek and modest. The whore is immodestly dressed, and her pouty lips announce her impure intentions.

Without question, the women decorating the covers of magazines and websites provide a powerful lure for the eyes of young men. Unless a young man identifies one of these women as a whore from the outset, he will likely be drawn into her sensual trap. Sadly, most young men will leap into these traps without hesitation. Today, easy accessibility to these prostitutes—whether real or imaginary—is almost universal, even though only a hundred years ago young men would have had to travel to large cities to access them.

Of course, there will always be local women of questionable character who will seduce men in their own schools or neighborhoods. Granted, there are plenty of men around who would seduce young ladies into sin, especially if these women are not secure and affirmed by their own fathers and brothers. Nevertheless, this proverb addresses the problem of the temptress who has an easier time seducing the average guy than men would in tempting a woman.

Family Discussion Questions:

1. Why is this warning about the whore so important for young men?

2. Why is this woman referred to as a "stranger"? What does she look like?

3. Where might young men find these whores?

PART 210 ~ THE POWERFUL LURE OF INTOXICATING SUBSTANCES
Proverbs 23:29–32

Who has woe? Who has sorrow? Who has contentions? Who has
  babbling? Who has wounds without cause? Who has redness of eyes?
They that tarry long at the wine; they that go to seek mixed wine.
Look not upon the wine when it is red, when it gives its color in the
  cup, when it moves itself aright.
At the last it bites like a serpent, and stings like an adder.

The Book of Proverbs catalogs the worst things that can happen
to men. It defines their sins and explains the sorriest miseries
that afflict mankind, of which alcohol addiction may be the
worst. Households cursed with the problem of drunkenness
are plagued by fighting, depression, accidents, and broken
relationships. Typically, drunks are incapable of conducting
meaningful relationships with their children. When a father
drinks too much alcohol, his children easily detect a change
in personality as he speaks with thick, slurred speech and
overwrought emotions. When he tells his children, "I love
you," they have a hard time believing him.

A great amount of abuse and murder in families comes about
because of drunkenness. In the sad history of family abuse,
so many men have come to regret the things they did while
under the influence of alcohol. Usually, after the deed is done,
they will insist they "didn't mean to do any of it." However,
once under the influence, they bring about many "wounds
without cause," and they then must face the consequences—a
lifetime of heartache!

Entire neighborhoods of lower-income homes in most
American cities today are made up of families like this. The
problem of drunkenness is so predictable in every place and
every generation since Adam that it seems hardly worth
mentioning. Where there are ruined families, wounded
hearts and lives, and broken economies, you will always find
communities of drunks, whether they be in Africa, Asia,

South America, or Nowhereville, Nevada. The differences lie only in the variety of drug or intoxicant available to the particular social group, with alcohol being the most common. For Muslims in Yemen, it may be Khat. For twenty-five-year-old Californians, it is marijuana or methamphetamines, while Afghani men are getting high on their heroin poppies. The problem is nearly universal. Billions of people around the globe are enslaved to these addictive substances, thus illustrating the inherent weakness of the human spirit wherever it is enslaved to its own lusts.

That is why a wise and concerned father would insert this warning into his book of wisdom. The last thing he wants is for his son to fall into this family-ruining trap.

The trap of drunkenness is a sort of spell. Something strange happens to the drunkard as he looks into the bottle of wine. He is completely controlled by it. All other values in life seem to dissipate in favor of the bottle. The true and living God fades, while this new god dominates his thoughts and affections. He is now willing to sacrifice his family's economic well-being, his relationships—everything—for the sake of the bottle. This is his god, and it is a horrible one. In the end, it takes the poor miserable creature into its arms and proceeds to beat him to death. *At the last it bites like a serpent, and stings like an adder.*

Family Discussion Questions:

1. What sorts of terrible things might a drunk do when he is under the intoxicating influences of alcohol?

2. How is the temptation to drunkenness a sort of spell that falls upon the drunkard?

3. What is the real sin underlying these addictions?

PART 211 ~ THE CURSE OF DRUNKENNESS
Proverbs 23:33–35

Your eyes shall behold strange women, and your heart shall utter
*   perverse things.*
Yea, you shall be as he that lies down in the midst of the sea, or as he
*   that lies upon the top of a mast.*
They have stricken me, shall you say, and I was not sick; they have
*   beaten me, and I felt it not: when shall I awake? I will seek it yet*
*   again.*

Drunkards do not produce godly fruit. They may write screenplays and great literature for the brave cities of men, but their thinking is twisted, nihilistic, depressed, and destructive. Most of the intellectuals of the last few centuries insisted that they could not have written the stuff they wrote without drinking copious amounts of alcohol in the process. This may be true, as their literature is a reflection of their lives. Most of these men lived in a way that was consistent with their writings, and then they ended their lives as Ernest Hemingway and Hunter S. Thompson did—by suicide.

The drunk gives up his family relationships for a strange woman, but he cannot feel what he is doing. With his judgment impaired while under the influence of alcohol, he runs his car over a cliff. After six months of recovery in the hospital, he emerges, only to return to the bottle. Drunkenness is a form of escape—like a sleep state—and herein lies the secret to its lure. By nature, men are running away from God. As they run, they must run from reality because reality is inescapably revelatory of God. Just as Adam and Eve hid from God in the garden, men will hide behind their drunken states, their fantasy novels, their electronic games, and an endless array of motion pictures. A man in this state doesn't feel the pangs of guilt when he is under the influence of alcohol. Of course, he isn't worshiping the true and living God in gratitude as he takes his fifteenth glass of booze, but he doesn't have to worry about this violation of the first commandment because his drunkenness closes off his ears to the cries of his conscience.

He cannot feel the emotional pain of losing his family relationships, the pangs of guilt, or the physical pain sustained by his accidents while under the influence of alcohol, so he has the best of all worlds! He can sin without guilt, hurt his body without suffering pain, and destroy his relationships without emotional repercussions. But one day he will awake to face reality as never before. The time will come when he will never be able to hide again from all the physical pain, emotional agony, and every imaginable spiritual torment. Unspeakably sad will be that day when he comes face to face with reality, and the most real experience of his life will occur when the Son of God says to him, "Depart from me, you cursed, you worker of iniquity." As sure as God is real, as the Lord lives, and as He is ever true to His absolutely just character, He will judge that man "to his face" (Deut. 5). On that day there will be no more whiskey, no more heroin, and no more escape ramps from the highway of reality as that man is carried into the flames of eternal fire.

But there is a refuge to be found from such a miserable end! For those who have ears to hear, there is hope if they will face the reality of God and His holy justice, of their sin, of Christ and His bloody atonement, and of God's grace. Granted, these are serious realities. People have a hard time accepting the reality of their sin and guilt and the painful consequences. But the alternative is fearful, unmentionable, and not even worth considering. So let us understand the fact that we are sinners who live in a sinful, fallen world. Then, let us receive the only possible solution to this terrible dilemma—God's salvation in His Son, Jesus Christ. Billions of others will try to escape these realities through alcohol and other opiates, and they will die in their sins. In this horrible predicament, how will we face these realities? Will we accept the only possible solution in this sin-cursed world? It is a solution that will repair family relationships, atone for our guilt, heal our diseases, and cure death with a resurrection. It is a grand solution! The brightest men of our generation solved their problems by intoxication and suicide, which are not solutions at all. For us, the only possible remedy is God's solution in the Lord Jesus Christ.

Family Discussion Questions:

1. What happens to a drunk's capacity to feel pain (both emotional and physical)?

2. Why do men want to escape into a dream-like state instead of facing reality?

3. Do you ever want to escape into the pretend worlds of novels, electronic games, motion pictures, or drunkenness? Instead of trying to escape reality, what should you do? How will you face the pain and effects of sin in this world?

To order other Family Bible Study Guides,
go to GenerationswithVision.com, call 1-888-839-6132,
or send an e-mail to mail@generationswithvision.com

~ ~ ~

The Bible is the Core Curriculum in the education of a child.
If we provide our children excellent academic instruction
in mathematics, science, and grammar, but neglect to teach
them Genesis, Psalms, Proverbs, and the Gospels, we have
failed in the education of our children.